BEFORE YOU THROW IN THE TOWEL

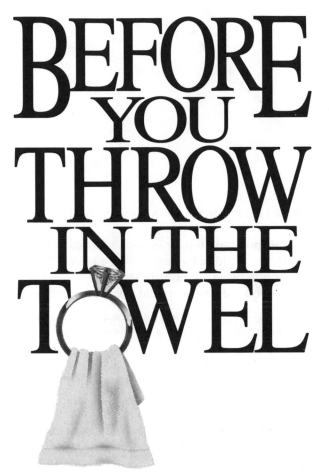

BEFORE YOU THROW IN THE TOWEL

12 THINGS YOU SHOULD CONSIDER BEFORE FILING FOR DIVORCE

DR. BOB MOOREHEAD

WORD PUBLISHING

Dallas · London · Vancouver · Melbourne

Library of Congress Cataloging-in-Publication Data

Moorehead, Bob
    Before you throw in the towel: twelve things you should consider
fore filing for divorce / Bob Moorehead.—1st ed.
    p. cm.
    Includes index
    ISBN 084–9934–575
    1. Marriage—United States. 2. Marriage—Religious aspe(
Christianity. I. Title
HQ734.M822   1992
646.78—dc20   91–40?
                                                                  CI

Printed in the United States of America.

97 96 95 94 93 92 LB 8 7 6 5 4 3 2 1

I humbly dedicate this book to
Gale and Carol Conner
whose example and tireless effort
have prevented scores of couples from
throwing in the towel.

——————— CONTENTS

_ ACKNOWLEDGMENTS

I want to thank Rick Albright, Bobbi McFadden, and Mary Young who helped in the word processing, printing, and the meeting of deadlines. I also want to thank my dear wife who helped proof and critique my material. I am also indebted to my children who as adults gave their opinions about hanging in till death in marriage.

_____ *INTRODUCTION*

M y seat was 14-F, an aisle seat on my flight from Seattle to Orange County. I had planned a two-hour time slot to get caught up on correspondence. So inundated with work, I did not notice who was seated across the aisle from me.

Once airborne, I dropped my tray and placed my notepaper on it. Just when I was ready to begin to write, a child's hand tapped me from across the aisle, and a voice barely above a whisper said, "Can you take me to the bathroom?" The voice was that of Jennifer, a five year old, seated next to her brother, Todd, a seven year old. They were traveling unaccompanied. I took Jennifer to the back of the plane, asked a flight attendant for help, and she took her to the bathroom. I instantly became Jennifer's friend and confidant for the next hour and a half. She and Todd talked constantly and told me their life history. The only part that touched me was this one statement made by Jennifer: "Our Seattle daddy and mommy are sending us to see our California daddy and mommy. Our California daddy is daddy George . . . our Seattle daddy is daddy Larry."

I asked them where they lived most of the time. They could not answer but said that during most of the school year they lived in Seattle. Their mother and father had been divorced two years ago, and their mother (in Seattle) was remarried to Larry. George, their real father, was remarried as well.

I closely observed those two kids (in between helping them to eat their lunch, getting them a pillow and a blanket, and escorting them to the toilet three more times). The lady sitting next to me, who had watched and heard the whole scenario, finally broke the silence on our side of the aisle to say, "Two more victims of our divorce-prone society!" How right she was.

Jennifer and Todd were extremely unsettled, nervous, undisciplined, and insecure. As the plane landed, they said to me, "Please don't walk too fast when you take us off the plane." That was the first I knew that I had been the one appointed to "take them off" the plane. By then my heart was broken for them. Do you know what broke my heart even more? "Daddy George" was not at the terminal to meet them. Their little faces dropped. As I handed them over to a flight attendant, I swallowed hard as they each gave me a hug, holding on for dear life! True, their father may have been caught in traffic, and his absence could have been no fault of his own. The fact remained, however, that it was one more event to unsettle their already unsettled lives. As I drove away from the airport with my host, I saw their little hands waving, and my heart broke again. I said to my host, "Two more tragic consequences of divorce!"

Chuck Swindoll says in *Strike the Original Match*, that in 1960 there were twenty-five divorces for every one hundred marriages; in 1975 there were forty-eight to every one hundred marriages.

Can anyone guess what the divorce statistics will be as we enter the twenty-first century? No one really wants to talk about it.

The county in which I live saw just under eight thousand divorces granted last year. Eight thousand times some judge dropped a gavel and said, *"Divorce Granted."*

"Our generation has been called the 'cut flower' generation. Nothing much lasts for very long."

Eight thousand times people broke their marriage vows. Eight thousand times couples and their attorneys bickered back and forth over who was going to get what. In about six thousand of those cases, a decision had to be made about child custody.

Our generation has been called the "cut flower" generation. Nothing much lasts for very long. Our "cartridge" philosophy advocates, "Don't repair it; discard it, and get another one." I recently saw a disposable camera put out by Kodak. You use it once, get the film developed, and pitch the cheap camera away. This "throw-away" thinking has drifted into marriage. "If it doesn't work out, get out of it, and get in a marriage that does work." Given this present day attitude toward marriage, it is no wonder that the divorce rate is escalating.

The purpose of this book is not to put divorced people on a guilt trip, nor to render judgments on the divorced, nor to establish a theology on divorce.

The purpose of this book is to say: Don't throw in the towel, or call it quits, or give it up. Your marriage may be going through a shredder at the moment. You may have been deeply hurt by the action of your spouse. But hold on! Before you file for divorce, take the time to read the following pages. It could change the course of your life and the lives of your children, if you have them. Hold on!

1

CONTEMPLATE
THE COMMITMENT

I will call them Ken and Louise. I was told by a friend of theirs that Ken was filing for divorce on Monday. One phone call and three hours later, Ken was in my office.

"It's true," he said with a long and shameful face, "Louise and I are at an impasse, and divorce is the only way out!"

There was no adultery involved. There were no big arguments, no violence, no major financial disagreements, no major sexual incompatibilities, no in-law troubles. When I pressed with the question "Why?" Ken calmly said, "Neither of us has any feelings left for the other anymore, and the civil thing to do is to give our marriage a decent burial."

Divorce is never "decent." Ken and Louise threw a perfectly good marriage down the drain because they mistakenly thought the glue that held it together was the glue of feeling.

Ken and Louise are not alone. Perhaps even as you read these lines, you can honestly say, "Whatever feelings I had for him (or her) have long since gone." And maybe you have concluded, "If the feeling is gone . . . the marriage is gone."

Now I will admit, there is something about early romance that "feels" good. Those "warm fuzzies" and "goose-bump" sensations of euphoria can be manifestations of our romantic love for someone. But while they may be one evidence that love is there, they are certainly not confirmations of love.

Love is a commitment, feelings or no feelings. Love is based on one's vow, one's word, one's promise. Feelings come and go, they rise and fall, they are frequent and infrequent. Commitment stays the same. The Scripture is clear about vows.

> When you make a vow to God, do not delay in fulfilling it. He has no pleasure in fools; fulfill your vow. It is better not to vow, than to make a vow and not fulfill it. (Ecclesiastes 5:4)

I asked Ken that day, "Don't you know you took a vow, and that vow is still in effect, regardless of your feelings toward Louise?" His response was the same one I have heard scores of times. "Yes, but things have changed since I made that vow." In effect, he was telling me that feelings can change a vow that was made. That is obviously how our culture thinks, especially when it comes to marriage vows. Let us examine those vows in the light of Ecclesiastes 5:4.

". . . to have and to hold . . ."

When a couple says those words to each other, they are words of ownership and permanence. There is a sense in marriage in which your spouse becomes yours, and you become his. That is why Paul says the following about the sexual union in marriage:

> The wife's body does not belong to her alone, but also to the husband. In the same way the husband's body does not belong to him alone, but also to his wife. (1 Corinthians 7:4)

The vow to "have and to hold" is a vow of a unique relationship.

". . . in sickness and in health . . ."

I add to that in my marriage ceremony, "in *good* times and in *bad* times." It is a vow that completely obligates me to my spouse, regardless of the circumstances, the changes in looks, shape, size, color of hair, presence or absence of hair, presence or absence of health, and presence or absence of mental faculties.

"Our commitment to our spouse is not kept or trashed on the basis of circumstances, but on the basis of 'is our word good?' "

One of the things Ken said to me was, "The Louise of today is not the Louise I married sixteen years ago." Part of that statement was true. She was twenty pounds heavier, her once dark brown hair was now heavily sprinkled with gray, and bifocals graced her face! But Ken was not the same either. His hair had gone through the four phases of hair on men: *hair, fuzz, is, wuz!*

Our commitment to our spouse is not kept or trashed on the basis of circumstances, but on the basis of "Is our word good?"

I vividly remember a dear couple in our congregation. When they were in their forties the wife came down with cancer. To keep the tumors from spreading, she had to have her leg amputated. Her husband stood by, encouraged, loved, helped, and supported her until her seemingly premature death after about eight months of suffering. He never flinched, nor did he ever give all that he did for her a second thought. He never even said, "I wish it weren't this way." When we expressed our love and compassion for both of them during her illness, which often times came across as pity for his lot too, he would say, "Well . . . we both said in sickness and in health . . . We enjoyed all those years of the health part, and this is the sickness part." What an attitude. His commitment did not waver when the circumstances shifted from good to bad.

". . . for better or for worse . . ."

A vow is a vow is a vow! It is a vow for the better times—my promise to stay by her, love her, and protect her during the good seasons. It is also a vow for the worse seasons when everyone is inconvenienced—expenses spiral, standards of living plummet, etc.

". . . for richer or for poorer . . ."

"Whatever comes, however long it stays, however tough it gets, we're in this thing together." Those are the only words of the song that I caught on my car radio one day. I do not know who scored the tune. It was not all that great, but those lyrics were "right on" when it comes to marriage!

One pastor recently told me he estimates that close to 50 percent of all divorces occur because of finances or the lack thereof. Maintaining a front of success has become so important for young couples that it places an inordinate amount of stress on the breadwinners who can never really measure up. I recently learned of a woman who left her husband because, in her words, "He's never been able to make a decent living the whole time we've been married." It was true that he had difficulty holding on to a good job very long, but is that a reason to break a vow and throw commitment to the wind? Not according to the Bible. Just because the "poorer" part of the vow had been present longer than the "richer" part of the vow does not give us the license to break it.

". . . till death do us part . . ."

This vow speaks of the duration of the commitment, which is until the death of one of the partners. Unfortunately, that word death is pronounced *debt* in some circles . . .

I stopped at a fast food place in southern California to get a soft drink. While in line, I noticed a very aged couple come in very slowly. Both were bent, holding onto each other, and moving with a great deal of caution. I could not resist. I walked over to them and said, "What a beautiful pair. . . . How long have you two been married?" He grinned, turned up his hearing aid, and asked me to repeat myself. I did. Then they both smiled and said, "It was June 1922. We remember it like it was yesterday." Then I said, "To what do you attribute the fact that you've stayed together this long?" His response was golden. "Why, we made a promise, and it's still good." Amen and Amen!

Why do we see the wholesale lack of commitment in marriage that causes couples to "bail out" when the going gets tough? I think there are some definite reasons.

Selfishness

Behind a broken vow is an attitude that says, "If I can't have it my way, I'll take my toys and go home." It is an attitude that bought into the marriage for what it could get instead of what it could give. This is true for men and women alike, but more often perpetrated by men. I've heard all the excuses:

- "She doesn't keep house the way she used to."

- "She's gained over twenty pounds since we were married."

- "She's not as romantic as she was at first."

- "She's slacked up in her cooking."

- "She doesn't keep herself as neatly as she did."

And on and on the complaining goes. If you have the ability to read between the lines of those complaints, you will readily see the monster of selfishness rearing its ugly head. One man going through a bitter divorce once said to me: "I believe if I'm going to provide an income of ninety-two thousand dollars a year and provide my wife with a nice home, car, and vacations, I'm entitled to a few things myself." That statement betrayed the presence of extreme selfishness in his life. Three words that should never be used by a married person in addressing his spouse are: *"I'm entitled to . . ."*

"Behind a broken vow is an attitude that says, 'If I can't have it my way, I'll take my toys and go home.' "

If you will reread the instruction manual on marriage for man and woman in Ephesians 5, you will notice there is not one bit of instruction that tells you to be in the marriage for what *you* can get out of it, but what your partner can get out of it.

The Excuse of Children

Believe it or not, when couples have children, the children are used by both spouses to break down their commitment to each other. For the woman it often expresses itself in the "bondage syndrome." The wife feels confined, trapped, obligated, over-burdened with the responsibilities and feels she is justified in bailing out of the marriage because her husband will not give her any help.

The man, on the other hand, sees the child or children as a rival, competing with him for the affection of the wife and mother. Yes, I grant you this is immaturity at its height, but it's often there. I have sealed in my counseling files many cases of marital infidelity that occurred within a few months after a first child was born, and in almost all of those cases the husband felt he was being left out and ignored by his wife, and that all of her affection was going to the new baby.

Agape love in the New Testament loves with no expectation of anything in return.

Biblical Rationalization

Some people slip out of their marital commitments today because they rationalize God's Word to accommodate their plans to divorce. Divorce among Christians today is almost as high as it is among non-Christians. Many of these people go back on their vow by saying, "Sure divorce is a sin, but no worse sin than anything else. . . . We live under grace, and God will forgive me. . . . God wants us happy, and if I can't be happy staying married, I don't think He'll condemn me for getting a divorce . . ." And so goes the myriad of mindless excuses for involving ourselves in something God absolutely hates, namely divorce! (Malachi 2:16).

God's word is perfectly clear. The *only* justifications for divorce in the Scriptures are: when an unbelieving partner leaves or divorces us (1 Corinthians 7:15–16); or when our spouse commits adultery (Matthew 19:9, 5:31–32).

The Mood of Our Culture

We live in a "slip-knot" civilization. A person's word is generally no longer good. Promises are broken, contracts are cancelled at whim, iron-clad agreements melt, and people go back on their word wholesale. Many warranties mean nothing, and are only as good as the integrity of the manufacturer. There has, in the past few years, been a serious erosion of commitment among employees in our country. There has also been a growing deficiency of commitment on the part of employers. Lack of commitment is all around us. Company loyalty is almost a thing of the past. So is a patriotic commitment to our country. In many evangelical churches, people go back on what they say they will do or give, and one wonders, "Where has old-fashioned follow-through-with-your-word gone?" So, when promises are broken at work, in government and in business, it is only a matter of time until this practice seeps like poison into marriages.

Endorsement by Others

Breaking the commitment of marriage today comes easier because even in Christian circles, the "stigma" attached to divorce is all but gone. Christians who go through a divorce often receive strokes of approval by their family, friends, and colleagues, even when those people are Christians.

Many churches have "divorce recovery" support groups, but I know of few churches with a "Divorce Strike Force Team" whose purpose it is to serve notice on Satan that he will not be successful with divorce.

I have been amazed by what I have heard from couples contemplating divorce: "We've prayed about this and feel that divorce is our only way out." It's like saying, "We now have the O.K. from God, so don't knock our divorce plans!"

On top of all this, the number of churches who dare to practice discipline against those who divorce for reasons forbidden by Scripture are miniscule. Such an attitude of "live and let live" existed in Corinth and came under condemnation by Paul:

> It is actually reported that there is immorality among you . . . and you are proud! Shouldn't you have been filled with grief? (1 Corinthians 5:1–2)

Where there is no restraint from the Christian community, no particular parameters, and no boundary lines, it makes it much easier to break the commitment of marriage.

So what is the solution? It is simple, really. We need to take our vow seriously. If you're contemplating a divorce even as you read these lines, please contemplate the commitment. God took you very seriously when you made that commitment, and so did your spouse. Do not look at your circumstances; do not enumerate the various ways you have been deprived or cheated; and do not justify your actions by appealing to your right to happiness and fulfillment. Stay true to your commitment, and regard it as God does, binding until death. By the way, you will be so glad you did!

2

CONSIDER THE COVENANT

T he sports car in front of me had the following sticker on its bumper: *"Too many marry for better or worse, but not for good."*

That statement is obvious. State laws governing divorce have greatly eased restrictions, making it easier than ever to procure a divorce. Most states are now no-fault divorce states. While browsing through a secular bookstore in Hawaii, I noticed a neatly packaged "Divorce Kit" with the sub-heading, "How to get a divorce without hiring an attorney . . . ten easy steps." (I doubt if the American Bar Association endorsed this kit!)

If you have been thinking about filing for divorce because of "irreconcilable differences," please consider the covenant first.

"Covenant" is not a household word today. In fact, we seldom use it in our everyday language. It sounds archaic, stoic, ancient, like it needs to be confined to antiquity. Most people do not realize that the original blueprint of marriage consisted of a three-way covenant between God, man, and the woman.

The Bible mentions several covenants: the old covenant; the Abrahamic covenant; the rainbow covenant, where God promised never to destroy the earth by water again; and the new covenant that Jesus established in the upper room. The covenant, however, that people do not talk about much is the marriage covenant.

It all started in Genesis when God said: ". . . it is not good for the man to be alone. I will make a helper suitable for him" (Genesis 2:18). The helper would be one who "fit," one who "matched." Interestingly enough, to get a perfect match God used as His base material a rib taken from Adam's side. Just as a bone-marrow transplant must come from a blood relative whose marrow "matches," so in marriage, part of the covenant was to find a person whose life "matched." In Genesis 2:24 it says, ". . . they will become one flesh." That one flesh is not only a sexual oneness, but a oneness marked by a special relationship called a "covenant."

Even when they sinned, God did not say, "Eve, you really messed up bad! I'm throwing you out and bringing someone else in for Adam." No, they were one flesh, and sin did not break that covenant, nor should it today. God keeps His covenants. "I will not violate My covenant or alter what my lips have uttered" (Psalm 89:34). Furthermore, according to Isaiah 24:5–6, God visited a curse on earth because His covenant had been broken. God takes covenants very seriously.

Jesus said, "So they are no longer two but one. Therefore what God has joined together, let not man separate" (Matthew 19:6). Ephesians 5:25ff tells us that the marriage covenant represents the same covenant that Jesus had with his church.

"The original blueprint of marriage consisted of a three-way covenant between God, man, and the woman."

Malachi 2 speaks of Judah's unfaithfulness in marrying the daughter of a foreign god. God called it "breaking faith." The writer goes on to say in that passage:

> Another thing you do: you flood the Lord's altar with tears. You weep and wail because he no longer pays attention to your offerings, or accepts them with pleasure from your hands. You ask "why?" It is because the Lord is acting as a witness between you and the wife of your youth, *because you have broken faith with her,* though she is your partner, the wife of your marriage covenant. (Malachi 2:13–14, emphasis added)

Here God plainly states that marriage is a covenant, one in which He is necessarily involved.

If you want a picture and description of an Old Testament marriage, reread Ezekiel 16.

> Later I passed by, and when I looked at you, and saw that you were old enough for love, I spread

the corner of my garment over you, and covered your nakedness. I gave you my solemn *oath* and entered into a *covenant* with you, declares the Sovereign Lord, and you became mine. (Ezekiel 16:8, emphasis added)

Though God is using this passage as an illustration of His relationship to His people, it reflects what a marriage relationship is built upon, namely, a covenant.

If one person breaks the marriage covenant and walks away from it, that still leaves two people in covenant, God and the other person. It only takes a simple majority to stand for the covenant. If you file for divorce, and your spouse decides to stand with God in covenant for the healing of your marriage, you could be fighting a losing battle.

Let us now return to Malachi. God's message gets strangely particular:

Has not the Lord made them one? In flesh and spirit they are his. And why one? Because he was seeking godly offspring. So guard yourself in your spirit, and do not break faith with the wife of your youth. *I hate divorce,* says the Lord God of Israel . . . (Malachi 2:14–16, emphasis added)

What is a "covenant?" It is an agreement. It is a pledge that we are in agreement with and supportive of the terms of the contract. If I buy a home, a contract is drawn up. I agree with the seller on a price, to put so much money down and to make a certain number of payments until the home is paid for, or until I sell it to someone else. We both sign the contract and thus enter into an agreed covenant.

In marriage a three-party contract is drawn up, with each party agreeing to do his part to make the contract valid and in force.

The Woman's Part of the Contract

The primary function of the wife is to ". . . submit to your husbands, as to the Lord. For the husband is the head of the wife, as Christ is the head of the church, his body, of which he is the Savior" (Ephesians 5:22, 23).

This really means only one thing. It means that upon entering the covenant, the woman agrees to the term that says her role is to acknowledge her husband as her head, not in an impersonal, dutiful, slave/master relationship, but as submitting to the structure which God has given marriage. What we have here is a form of "chain of command." But that term does not mean the wife is in chains, and the husband is in command! Absolutely not.

Connected with this relationship is another injunction that is a term of the covenant. "To the married I give this command (not I but the Lord) a wife must not separate from her husband" (1 Corinthians 7:10).

Wives, you are commanded by God, as a part of the covenant relationship to which you agreed, *Do not leave your husband.* That really is not hard to understand but often times very hard to obey.

The Man's Part of the Contract

The husband, likewise, is called upon to fulfill one major responsibility in the covenant: "Husbands, love your wives just as Christ loved the church, and gave himself up for her . . . " (Ephesians 5:25). While the wife is called upon to love her husband enough to live for him, the husband is called upon to love his wife enough to die for her. What a great thought!

Men are also called to fulfill another term of the covenant. "And a husband must not divorce his wife" (1 Corinthians 7:11b).

What if the covenant is broken by either the wife or the husband? Does that mean the covenant can never be put back together? Not at all. Sin is forgivable (1 John 1:9). As already stated, the only two reasons Christians may be permitted to end a marital relationship are: (1) your spouse commits adultery or, (2) your unbelieving spouse abandons the marriage on his/her own. Even then, the covenant does not have to be broken. Your forgiveness of their sin, and your determination to stand for the healing and restoration of the covenant relationship takes precedence over your "right" to divorce. Marriages are not automatically broken because of sexual unfaithfulness.

≈ ≈ ≈

If marriage is a covenant relationship, we need to remember some very important things.

1. God Takes Very Seriously Any Covenant In Which He Participates

The Old Testament is full of the judgments of God after the point at which God passes judgment on

> ## "While the wife is called upon to love her husband enough to live for him, the husband is called upon to love his wife enough to die for her."

Judah and Israel for breaking their covenant with God. If we break the covenant of marriage, we will be forced to live with the consequences. Covenants are made to be honored, not set aside.

2. The Covenant of Marriage Is Just As Sacred as the New Covenant Under Which All Believers Live

Many mistakenly think that the only covenant in force today is the New Covenant which was sealed and ratified by the blood of Christ. Wrong. It is in effect, but so is the covenant of marriage if we have entered into that covenant. God did not change the terms of the covenant of marriage from the Old Testament to the New Testament.

3. To Break the Covenant of Marriage Is To Greatly Dishonor the One Who Initiated The Covenant in the First Place

It goes without saying that to break the marital covenant by filing for divorce is to completely dishonor

God, who initiated the covenant to begin with. It is a frank admission that somehow God was wrong in initiating that covenant, or that He initiated a faulty, less than perfect covenant. To break it is to arrogantly suggest that we somehow have a superior plan.

4. To Break the Covenant of Marriage Is To Say That My Assessment of the Problem Of My Marriage Is More Accurate and Greater Than God's Solution

To file for divorce is to acknowledge that your marriage is so damaged that not even God can do anything about it. It is a step in the direction of denying the omnipotence of God.

ᶻᵃ ᶻᵃ ᶻᵃ

So, before you file for divorce, consider the covenant, consider the initiator of the covenant, consider the binding nature of that covenant, and the consequences of breaking that covenant. In retrospect, someday you will look back and say, "Thank God I honored and respected the covenant."

---------------------------------- *3*

PUNCTURE
THE PRIDE

F rank was nervous as he spilled his guts about his wife. A car repair shop owner, he had just celebrated his thirty-eighth birthday. He and Vera had two children, twelve and fourteen. It was a story not unlike many I have heard, yet the anger, pain, and disappointment all blended together as he spilled it all out with a great deal of emotion.

It all started when Vera went to work part-time for a young attorney, at first doing word processing for depositions. She worked three hours on Monday, Wednesday, and Thursday evenings while Frank watched the children. The job provided a good pay, and the added income helped with all the expenses of orthodontics and the other increasing financial demands of teens.

Soon Vera was asked by her boss to work twenty hours per week, coming in at 4:00 P.M. and staying until 8 P.M., five days a week. He offered more per hour plus benefits, and Frank had reluctantly given his consent. The young attorney took on another partner, George, age thirty-six, recently divorced. He often worked on into the evenings, and he and Vera

would eat a sandwich together. This led to an occa-
sional after work meal. Eventually, feelings began to
develop between the two. As affairs go, in series of
progressions, George kissed Vera one night before
she left the office. Now she was emotionally involved, yet felt incredibly guilty. Another week of
this led to George inviting her to his apartment for a
drink or two. Suddenly Vera realized how easily she
was becoming emotionally attached. She wanted to
do it; her feelings were strong. But realizing what she
would throw away, she literally grabbed her purse
and ran out of the office. Risking Frank's anger and
maybe even his leaving her, she went home, took
him into the back yard, and divulged the whole affair, reassuring him that she had not committed adultery, though she had come close.

She was not prepared for Frank's reaction. He
jumped to his feet, ran into the house, packed all he
could get into his gym bag, and left. He stayed in a
local motel, and the next day rented an apartment. In
spite of her repeated attempts at reconciliation, and
her endless requests for his forgiveness, Frank's jaw
was set.

He consulted his attorney, and within a week,
drew up divorce papers. On his way home from the
attorney's office, he called to see me. As a member of
our church, Frank was not very active, but he did
attend every Sunday. As he sat across from me, he
trembled, partly with anger, partly with fear, and
partly with remorse. I really think he came to see me
to get me to condone his actions.

"I have a right . . ." he spoke in a loud tone. "That's one thing I won't tolerate, an affair." After reminding him that he did not have biblical grounds for divorce, I proceeded to work on his number one

---

"The Bible has a lot to say about pride, and nowhere does pride rear its ugly head more than in marital relationships."

---

problem . . . *pride.* His manly pride had been offended, and in the whole process he was thinking about only one person, *himself.* Though he softened a bit, he was still intent on filing for divorce, throwing seventeen years of marriage down the tube because his wife made a mistake. In spite of knowing he would face church discipline, Frank left, not quite as adamant, but still saying he was going through with a divorce because he could never trust Vera again. His problem was a classic problem of pride.

As a spouse, maybe your pride has been offended by an action on the part of your spouse. The Bible has a lot to say about pride, and nowhere does pride rear its ugly head more than in marital relationships.

What is pride? It is an inflated sense of importance about ourselves that always stands in the way of wholesome relationships. Where people are extremely proud and have no sense of condescending, you can bet it will breed broken relationships in their marriage. "Pride only breeds quarrels, but wisdom is found in those who take advice" (Proverbs 13:10).

We have all heard the passage which says that "Pride goes before destruction, and a haughty spirit before a fall" (Proverbs 16:18). Solomon was also wise enough to say: "A man's pride brings him low . . ." (Proverbs 29:23). Paul says in 1 Corinthians 13:4 that love is not proud. James 4:6 says, "God opposes the proud, but gives grace to the humble." We are told in Scripture to "Humble yourselves, therefore under God's mighty hand, that he may lift you up in due time" (1 Peter 5:6).

Frank's character weakness really manifested itself when something happened between him and Vera which gave it a chance to surface. I have found that behind almost every divorce in which I have been personally involved and know some of the facts, pride is ultimately the culprit. No one is worse to be around than a person whose pride has been wounded.

Look with me at some of the aspects of pride and see if it is afflicting your life and creating a barrier in your marital relationship.

The Source of Pride

The source of all pride is found in an inflated and exaggerated view of one's self. Frank assumed, by his refusal to forgive Vera, that he would never or could never do such a thing. The fact is, he could, and should!

We all need to return from time to time to the exhortation of Scripture:

Do not think of yourself more highly than you ought but rather think of yourself with sober judgment . . . (Romans 12:3)

In these days when we are constantly being told that we need large doses of "self-esteem," is it any wonder that so many people have developed a false assessment of themselves?

This is not to say that we need to downgrade ourselves, put ourselves down, and always openly confess that we are unworthy, unclean, and undeserv-

> ## "Pride never allows us to forgive or show compassion for those who have made mistakes."

ing, though as relates to our salvation, all of that is true. It does mean that we are not above forgiving others when they have wronged us. Pride never allows us to forgive or show compassion for those who have made mistakes.

Pride Often Reveals Rigid Legalism

When puffed up with pride, we are operating in the arena of legalism, not mercy. Mercy and pride are like oil and water; they never mix. Pride assumes that we have no place in our lives for the mistakes of others. Legalists base their relationships on rules, standards, edicts, and lists. When one of those is violated, too bad. You must pay for your sin; you must, like a worm, crawl your way back into the relationship.

Jesus was terse with legalists in His day. He upbraided the teachers of the law for their legalistic approach to life:

> Woe to you, teachers of the law and Pharisees, you hypocrites! You give a tenth of your spices, mint, dill and cumin. But you have neglected the more important matters of the law—justice, mercy, and faithfulness. *You should have practiced the latter without neglecting the former.* (Matthew 23:23, emphasis added)

Dill seed is about as small as seeds come, yet they would use up valuable time counting out a tithe of that seed to make sure they did not give too much! For them there was no margin for error in their dealings with other people either.

Frank's attitude came off much like the Pharisees. You break the rules, you pay the piper, and that's that! I wondered while we talked if he had ever read the story of the woman caught in adultery. The Pharisees brought her to Jesus and demanded that she be stoned because that was what the Law called for in such cases. Jesus thinned the crowd by saying, "Let him who is without sin cast the first stone." That was one rock festival that never got off the ground; they all left. Then He said to her that neither did He condemn her and for her to go and sin no more. Our God is the God of second and third chances!

Pride Usually Reveals the Lack Of a Humble Heart Toward God

When a person's pride will not allow him or her to forgive offenders, it usually reveals that he/she is also proud in his/her relationship to God. Horizontal pride usually confirms a vertical pride. God honors humility but hates a haughty spirit. "I live in a high and holy place, but also with him who is contrite and lowly in spirit" (Isaiah 57:15).

By the same token it would be well for all of us to recognize the person God esteems. We hear much today about "self-esteem" and "vocational-esteem," but what about "God-esteem?"

> This is the one I esteem: he who is humble and contrite in spirit, and trembles at my word. (Isaiah 66:2)

A hard heart is always created by pride. It is pride's by-product. Once the Pharisees came to Jesus to find out if he thought a person could divorce his wife for "any" cause. They reminded Jesus that Moses "permitted" a man to write a certificate of divorce and dismiss her (Deuteronomy 24). Jesus' response is classic:

> Moses permitted you to divorce your wives because your hearts were hard. But it was not this way from the beginning. (Matthew 19:8)

The Pharisees were trying to justify a practice which was caused by hardness of heart. God had told them in the Old Testament that since they were rebellious and had a hard heart to not forget the paper work when they divorced.

I have talked with scores of divorcees who have confided in me that they would still be married today had they been willing to puncture their pride and humble themselves before their mate.

Men especially struggle with humbling themselves before their wives, fearing they will lose some of their "leadership" and "manhood" if they eat crow. Many men feel that it is emasculating and a sign of weakness to extend a hand of forgiveness to their wives. To the contrary, it takes a real man to be willing to have an accurate view of himself and to humble himself before his mate.

If your mate has offended you in any way, either by an affair, or in any other way, reach out and love him, forgive him, and let him know that though you were hurt by it all, you love him, and pray that he'll have the same attitude toward you if you ever drop the ball.

I am glad to report that at the eleventh hour, Frank woke up to smell the coffee . . . went to Vera . . . asked her forgiveness for the way he acted, and today they are one of the happiest and most fulfilled couples I know. It would have been another gruesome divorce statistic otherwise.

If you are the offended one, why not pray this prayer right now and make it your own:

Lord, I confess my pride to You right now. Cleanse me from all ostentation, arrogance, and inflated ego. Give me the strength to forgive, to love, to accept, and to humble myself before my spouse. Amen.

There is no place for pride in the Christian life. Jesus humbled himself and became obedient to the point of death. The Bible also says he learned obedience through what he suffered (Hebrews 5:8). He is our example. Pride and marriage cannot co-exist. So, before you file for divorce, humble yourself before your spouse. God's plan works!

4

BURY THE BITTERNESS

E very time the judge drops the gavel and says, "Divorce granted," it is confirmation of the fact that somewhere along the line, someone, somehow, in some way refused to forgive his/her spouse.

From time to time we will hear about another movie star who has filed for divorce stating "irreconcilable differences." A movie has even been made with that title. Of course, the differences are irreconcilable because one or both spouses refuses to reconcile . . . not because the differences *can't* be reconciled. Where pride leaves off, bitterness begins. . . .

If you have never sat in a divorce court or a preliminary hearing chamber . . . don't! That is, unless you want your day or your entire week to be ruined. The vehemence, vindictiveness, hatred, and animosity that exude from both spouses and their attorneys put enough poison in the air to pollute an entire city.

Most, if not all, divorces are predicated on an offense or a series of offenses one or both parties are unwilling to forgive. Not even the well being of small children or the pleading of a couple's parents can dissuade, in most cases, an offended spouse. Bitterness and resentment breed bitterness and resentment. Like a malignant cancer they spread rapidly and with great destruction until it becomes almost impossible for the offended to forgive. The offended is usually not just one spouse. By the time a divorce is filed for, both spouses have become "the offended."

Perhaps as you read these lines, you are contemplating a divorce, or maybe you have already filed or have been filed upon. Before you proceed a step further, let me remind you of the destructiveness of bitterness and the refusal to forgive. Following are some consequences that come when bitterness is not buried.

Bitterness Causes Poor Physical, Emotional, And Mental Health

You may not notice it now or feel it now, but refusal to forgive takes a terrific toll on your all around health. Because bitterness and grudge holding are sins (not just passing problems), until they are resolved, you are likely to suffer stomach pains and irregularities, insomnia, headaches, high blood pressure, loss of appetite, and unclear thinking.

David sinned with Bathsheba and tried to cover the sin with the murder of her husband. He held this sin inside himself but paid the price. He finally released it and wrote his testimony about it in Psalm thirty-two.

When I kept silent, my bones wasted away through my groaning all day long. For day and night your hand was heavy upon me; my strength was sapped as in the heat of summer. (Psalm 32:4)

In short, David was miserable. No peace of mind, no joy, no lilt, no health, just a miserable existence.

"A divine catharsis occurs in open confession. It is like lancing a boil. . . . It is painful, . . . but what healing follows the pain!"

He went to bed with it and woke up with it; it was eating him alive. Now listen!

Then I acknowledged my sin to you and did not cover up my iniquity. I said I will confess my transgressions to the Lord, and you forgave the guilt of my sin. (Psalm 32:5)

A divine catharsis occurs in open confession. It is like lancing a boil full of poisonous puss which is polluting the blood stream. It is painful to lance it, but what healing follows the pain!

A physician once said to me that almost every illness he knows is made worse by unresolved conflict in people's lives, and in some cases their illness is caused by locked-in bitterness and a refusal to forgive.

Bitterness Blocks Your Prayers

Harboring bitterness is too large a price to pay when you consider that it results in God turning a deaf ear to our prayers. "And when you stand praying, *if you hold anything against anyone,* forgive him, *so that* your Father in heaven may forgive your sins" (Mark 11:25, emphasis added).

Part of our prayer life is confession of sin; and if we refuse to confess that sin of bitterness and do something about it, we have just blocked God's forgiveness of *our* sins. This does not mean that we *earn* our forgiveness by forgiving others; it just means that God will not forgive an unforgiving heart. If God did forgive an unforgiving heart, He would, in effect, be condoning bitterness.

The Bible is also clear that unless husbands treat their wives with respect and consideration, their prayers are greatly hindered:

> Husbands, in the same way be considerate as you live with your wives, and treat them with respect as the weaker partner, and as heirs with you of the gracious gift of life, so that nothing will hinder your prayers. (1 Peter 3:7)

It is clear that the harboring of bitterness greatly affects our spiritual lives, doing damage that may very well not be repaired. Perhaps this is why Solomon wisely wrote:

> A man's wisdom gives him patience; it is to his glory to overlook an offense. (Proverbs 19:11)

Harboring Resentment
Presumes You Are Superior
To the Offender

Now you may counter with, "No, I'm not superior. I just can't forgive what she or he has done, and I don't want to live with that kind of person again."

But wait! What about the exhortation in Scripture that says:

> Be kind and compassionate to one another, forgiving each other, *just as in Christ, God forgave you.* (Ephesians 4:32, emphasis added)

Refusal to forgive another attempts to cancel out the fact that God has forgiven you. When you stop and think of all that you have been forgiven by God, you will have much less trouble forgiving your spouse. In refusing to forgive what we really do is

> ## "In refusing to forgive what we really do is set ourselves up to be higher than God."

set ourselves up to be higher than God. In other words God forgave us, but we won't forgive our fellow man. There is nothing your spouse has done to offend you that is greater than what you have done to offend God.

Bitterness Keeps Us
From Worshiping God

Part of the consequence of harboring grudges is an aborted worship life. Worship of God is at the core of our being. When we cease to worship, we cease to live. In His Sermon on the Mount, Jesus stressed the seriousness of anger and bitterness toward our fellow man, then goes on to say how bottled-up resentments and anger make us ineligible to worship God:

> But I tell you that anyone who is angry with his brother will be subject to judgment . . . Therefore if you are offering your gift at the altar, and there remember that your brother has something against you, leave your gift there in front of the altar. First go and be reconciled to your brother, then come and offer your gift. (Matthew 5:22–24)

It is interesting that Jesus said, "your brother has something against you," instead of "you have something against your brother." His point is this: Any breach in a relationship must be mended, or worship cannot take place. This is nowhere truer than in marriage.

Any offense we refuse to forgive has a tendency to harden us in all our other relationships. "An offended brother is more unyielding than a fortified city" (Proverbs 18:19).

I have discovered that in cases where I could not talk a person out of filing for divorce, bitterness was usually carried right over into the next marriage and caused the same damage there that it did in the first marriage. Resentment is also contagious. Others are greatly affected even when they are not the cause of the offense.

All of our future decisions are colored and hampered by our refusal to forgive.

When the Bible says, "Love covers a multitude of sins," (1 Peter 4:8) it is true. Real agape love has a way of covering offenses.

The emphasis here to forgive and bury your bitterness in no way condones the offender or the offense. It does, however, extend the same compassion to our spouse that God has extended to us.

ぬ ぬ ぬ

If you are contemplating divorce, or have already filed for divorce, please recall the greatest forgiveness story in the Bible. We call it the story of the prodigal son. It is recorded in the fifteenth chapter of Luke, and tells of a young man who was obviously not getting along with his father. He asked for an early advance on his inheritance and split the scene. His new found freedom, however, turned out to be his new found "bondage." Stripped of money, clothing, food, shelter, and now any sense of self worth, he found himself doing the lowliest of all jobs just to hold skin and bone together, a feed flinger on a pig farm. It was then that he decided his father's servants fared better than he, so he set out for home. I am sure that the closer he got, the more nervous he became. He fully expected reproach, chastisement, and sternness from his father; but to his surprise, his father saw him from a distance and embraced him then honored him with a feast. He was restored. Forgiveness covered his sin.

Have you ever wondered why he went down the spiral so quickly on the outside? It was not because he could not get a job or did not have the skill to hold a job. It was because bitterness was eating him alive. It always makes a pauper out of its victims. It is unrelenting and a cruel taskmaster to serve.

Whatever has angered you about your spouse, whatever offense he or she has committed, whatever breach that offense has caused, it is not too late to forgive and restore the relationship.

For you personally, the option of reconciliation may seem remote at this point and maybe even undesirable. But may I remind you . . . the alternative is worse. It has consequences that I am not sure you want to live with the rest of your life.

In a retreat setting I once asked all the singles who had been through a divorce to write anonymously on a piece of paper whether or not, if they had it to do again, they would forgive their spouse and refuse to divorce. Over 95 percent of them responded with a resounding *Yes.* O, the accuracy of hindsight!

Before you file for divorce, please bury the bitterness. You'll be so glad you did. And so will God.

5

SUBMERGE THE SELFISHNESS

I f divorce has its roots in pride and bitterness, it also has its roots in selfishness. The fact is, every divorce pivots around self-centeredness, egoism, and selfish motives. If a marriage is built on selfishness, divorce will be the inevitable consequence.

Meeting "My" Needs

Though not his real name, I will call him Randy. I remember their wedding. You would have had difficulty convincing me that less than three years later, he and Michelle would be going through divorce proceedings. She came to me in tears to say that he had moved out and was hanging around with his old buddies, all of whom sympathetically encouraged him to "get out of his marriage" so he could have happiness and fulfillment. After several attempts to talk with Randy (I was the last person on earth he wanted to see), we were finally able to meet. With a look of sincerity and a quasi-"righteous" tone in his voice, he proceeded to tell me how "deprived" he had been in their three years of marriage. He began his list.

- "She is definitely not meeting my sexual needs . . ."

- "After I work ten hours a day, half the time I come home to no meal prepared and a messy house."

- "When I want to go hunting or fishing, she pouts, and I spend all week trying to make up."

"She's not meeting my needs." Sound familiar? Those words are continually echoed by husbands and wives all over our land and become the prelude to the divorce court.

Randy had gone as far as contacting an attorney whose name had been given by a friend who was in the final stages of a divorce himself. It is amazing that when you start talking divorce, there is always a friend (?) who stands ready to give you an attorney's phone number.

Most people who initiate a divorce do so because they are not getting what they want. Their "needs" are just not being met.

Someone has said that the first three causes of divorce are:

1. Selfishness
2. Selfishness
3. (you guessed it) *Selfishness!*

Of course, ours is a culture centered on self. Magazines on the self abound at check-out counters. Check any book store and you will find a plethora of paperbacks dealing with looking out for number one. People apply for jobs asking, "What's in it for me?" People join the service asking, "What's in this for me?" Many join social clubs looking for self-gratification.

We live in the age of "rights." We hear someone say, "I have my rights" almost every day. I seldom hear anyone say, "I have my responsibilities."

Nowhere is selfishness more rampant than in marriage. People begin to focus on the question, "What am I getting out of this marriage?"

Through a series of meetings, I was able to help Randy discover the real purpose of marriage. Fortunately, when his eyes eventually came off of Randy and got placed on Jesus Christ then Michelle, he abandoned the idea of divorce, and they re-united, this time on an altogether different basis. This is not to dismiss Michelle's deficiencies. When he got his focus off his own needs, she got hers on them!

A Solid Basis

There are really only two bases on which a marriage can be built:

1. The "What can I do for you?" basis.
2. The "What can you do for me?" basis.

Let us look at the last basis first. This spouse sees marriage *only* as a way to gratify his or her needs and as a way to move toward fulfillment. Now, no one will argue that we all have needs: sexual needs, the need for companionship, and the need to be loved. Let us also admit that marriage, at its highest level, more than fulfills those needs in us. However, the man or woman who enters marriage with the idea of getting their needs met, rather than meeting their mate's needs is in for a heartbreaking experience. He is entering marriage at the level of selfishness. It is a matter of primary focus.

If you were to ask many men, "What is the purpose of your spouse?", you might get some answers like these:

- To sexually satisfy my strong sex drive.

- To fill the void of loneliness and be a companion to me.

- To do domestic things for me like cooking, sewing, and cleaning.

- To help with the family expenses by working part or full time.

- To be an attractive companion with me at company functions.

- To take care of the kids, buy their clothes, get them to their dental appointments, etc.

- To do some household functions that I do not have time to do.

Where does the list end? If you study that list again, you will notice that it is a self-serving list. He is the served, and she is the servant!

If your marriage has been based on "What can she do for me?", there will inevitably come a time when your spouse will not measure up, drop the ball, and will fail you. No one can stay on the performance wheel week in and week out without skipping a beat.

> **"The man or woman who enters marriage with the idea of getting their needs met, rather than meeting their mate's needs is in for a heartbreaking experience."**

Most wives will fulfill all of the functions listed above because their focus is on serving their husbands, not because they are given a quota and must perform.

Selfishness is at the center of the "What-can-my-spouse-do-for-me?" basis. And because the expectations are wrong, the performance will eventually fail; and the marriage will be over because it was predicated on selfishness and greed.

On the other hand, if your marriage is based on the "What-can-I-do-for-my-spouse?" basis, not only are the unmet expectations removed, but the emphasis is in the right place—serving instead of being served. Your questions will change to these:

- How can I meet my *spouse's* sexual needs?

- What can I do to make my *spouse's* life easier?

- How can I give my *spouse* a sense of worth?

- In what ways can I bring encouragement to my *spouse?*

Encouragement from Scripture

We are all prone to selfishness. Self-preservation is a strong instinct in all of us. But we are warned again and again in Scripture to avoid it like the plague: "Do nothing out of selfish ambition or vain conceit . . ." (Philippians 2:3). When selfishness enters a marriage, disintegration is not far away. "For where you have envy and selfish ambition, there you find disorder and every evil practice" (James 3:16).

A key verse that could cancel a thousand divorces today if it were read and practiced is taken from Philippians 2:4: "Each of you should look not only to your own interests but also to the interests of others."

If you will go back and read the marriage instructions in Ephesians 5 and Colossians 2, you will notice that they are given in the context of *responsibilities*, not *rights and privileges.* In other words, Paul does not say, "Okay wives, you make sure your husband loves you like Christ loves the church . . . and if he doesn't here's what you ought to do . . ." No, instead

Paul gives wives an injunction to submit to their husbands (Ephesians 5:22).

When it comes to the husband, Paul's injunction does not read, "Okay, men, your job is to see to it that your wife is submissive so all your needs will be met, and if she isn't, here's what you need to do . . ." No, Paul gives a clear command for the husband to assume the responsibility to love his wife like Christ loved the church (Ephesians 5:25).

If you are contemplating divorce because you are not getting what is coming to you, whether you are the wife or the husband, please get your focus off of your unmet needs and shift the focus to fulfilling your responsibilities.

Don't Keep Score

One of the most destructive things in marriage is keeping score. "I've given in three times this week, and she hasn't given in once yet!" or, "I've done what she wanted to do four times this month, and she hasn't done but one thing I wanted to do." Do not compare, do not keep score, do not keep a running tally of the times your needs went unmet. Nobody wins in an exercise like that.

Before you even think of going through with a divorce, ask yourself the following questions:

- Has my major focus been on meeting my spouse's needs rather than mine?

- Has my selfishness contributed to our growing apart?

- Am I willing to throw away a marriage for the sake of my selfishness?

- Am I willing now to try again, this time focusing on my spouse's needs instead of how my spouse is not meeting my needs?

Crucify your selfishness and submerge it! You will be so glad you did.

6

CHECK OUT
THE CHILDREN

T he voice at the other end of the phone was quiv-
ering. It was a man whose profession of faith I
had heard when he and his wife had given themselves to Christ twelve years ago. We'll call him
Devin. "My wife is filing for divorce, and my world
is coming apart." In the course of the conversation,
Devin confided that he and his wife had problems in
their marriage from day one, and that within three
years of their marriage, they had talked of divorce.
He told me that both he and his wife deliberately put
it off for the sake of the children. But now that their
children were fifteen and thirteen, in Devin's words,
"At least they won't be so devastated now that
they're older." Little did he realize just how devastating a divorce is to children, regardless of their age.

There is a myth going around that says, "Children are not a legitimate reason for a couple to stay
together." One secular counselor told a couple that
they must make their decision on divorce apart and
beyond the feelings of their children. What sad advice. Whose act of love caused those children to be
conceived? Who took care of them, fed them, clothed

them, educated them . . . it was the parents. If there is any valid reason for a couple to stay together besides the biblical mandate to not divorce, it certainly ought to be the presence of children. Divorce devastates children, whether they are pre-school age, grade school age, teens, or college age. Even if they are grown and married, the effect is felt full force.

Before you file for divorce consider what divorce does to children, whether they are six months, eight, eighteen, or twenty-eight years old.

1. Divorce Shatters Stability in the Minds Of Your Children

Regardless of age, your child or children receive the largest part of their stability and security from the solid marriage they have observed. It is their primary security blanket. Though many things in their lives change, and they are assaulted by the society of which they are a part, their parents' marriage is the one thing that they count on to stay solid and secure. When that relationship goes, their esteem falls, their confidence lessens, and their effectiveness as a person decreases. Nothing in their world is as important for their sense of well-being as the healthy marriage of their parents.

2. Divorce Forces Your Children To Take Sides

Outwardly your children may successfully hide it, but make no mistake about it, they are forced to

> ## "Divorce devastates children, whether they are pre-school age, grade school age, teens, or college age."

choose sides. I have had teens and older children tell me over and over that when their parents finally divorced, they hated having to show partiality to one over the other. Children should never be put in that kind of position.

3. Divorce Creates a Distrust in Some Children of Their Parents

A sense of betrayal is experienced in children of all ages when their parents go through a divorce. They feel embarrassed to let anyone know, and they feel ashamed when others find out. Their reasoning goes like this: "If my parents can't be trusted to tough it out in thick and thin, what can I trust them to do?" Any way you stack it, their trust of you and in you is shattered in a divorce. Try as you may, say what you will, but do not expect the level of their trust in you to remain the same.

4. Divorce Creates a Suspicion in Children

Children of divorcees become suspicious of entering into serious relationships with people of the opposite sex for fear that they may experience the same thing some day. They become highly suspicious of their girlfriends or boyfriends and their motives. For many children, it makes them "gun shy" of marriage. It makes them suspicious of marriage itself and may delay their getting married, if at all.

5. Divorce Creates Bitterness and Animosity Against One or Both Parents

While this is not true in every case, it is true in too many. Respect is lost, and it becomes very difficult for the child to continue to honor his/her parents. This resentment is often carried right over into the child's own marriage.

6. Divorce Easily Creates a Generational Divorce Pattern

Studies have shown that a very large percentage of younger couples who file for divorce had parents that were divorced. Today we are witnessing third generation divorces. No, divorce is not genetically "inherited," but the chances of your child getting a divorce someday is significantly raised if you have "set the example," so to speak.

Yes, divorce seriously affects your child, maybe even to "the third and fourth generation."

Most couples never stop to consider what their divorce means from the perspective of their children:

- Their weddings are seriously affected in the future.

- All future birthday gatherings are awkward. Can both parents attend, especially if they are remarried by then?

"Studies have shown that a very large percentage of younger couples who file for divorce had parents that were divorced."

- Attendance at graduations and awards banquets become awkward and embarrassing.

- The birth of your child's first baby is an awkward time for "grandma and grandpa."

- Holidays and special events become delicate times, especially when spouses remarry.

7. Divorce Brings a General Sense of Embarrassment to Your Child

What will children tell their friends, cousins, Sunday School teacher, and school teacher? Think about their feelings. Before you file for divorce, please check with your children.

Psalm 127:3 tells us that children are a heritage and reward from the Lord. If that is true, should they not be seriously considered before filing for the end of a marriage? In fact, when you stop and think about it, what better reason to stay married than for your offspring? I can think of none. If you put the issue to a vote by your children, guess how they would cast their ballots?

Maybe as you read these lines, you are reasoning: "We're in mid-life, our children are grown and most have families of their own, so our divorce will have a minimal affect on them." Think again! In some ways the pain and agony of having your parents split up after you are grown and married not only presents an embarrassment, but makes it very hard for your children to explain the divorce to their children. Part of your grandchildren's normal development is having a healthy relationship with their grandparents, and seeing in them a model for marriage. It is one thing if that is missed because one of their grandparents is deceased or lives elsewhere, but quite another if they are divorced.

We're seeing a generation come on the scene today whose grandparents divorced, parents divorced, and the odds are favorable that they will develop that same divorce pattern. Once a generational divorce pattern begins, it is very hard to break. But it can be done by refusing to entertain the thought of divorce.

Most couples do not want to "burden" their children with their marital woes. In most divorce cases involving couples forty-five years old and over, the

parents have never talked with their children concerning their marital problems. I believe this is a vio-
lation of family trust that is part and parcel of famil-
ial relationships. If we cannot talk with our family,
with whom can we talk and seek counsel? Consult
your children. Give them credit for being willing to
listen and make a good response.

8. Divorce Creates a Rootlessness in Your Children

Every family has family traditions, favorite foods,
family functions, family heirlooms, recipes, places,
and events that give children a sense of having roots.
Divorce tends to shatter these.

A young couple in our church sat across from my
desk in tears over the fact that the wife's parents
were filing for divorce. As she sat there enumerating
all the traditions she had enjoyed with her parents
over the years, I could see the sense of despair on her
face as she said, "All of those things that meant so
much . . . going down the tube when the judge says,
'divorce granted.'" This family had a little tradition
of gathering for a family barbecue every Friday
night, even after the daughter had married. Another
tradition consisted of going out to eat breakfast every
Easter Sunday after church. The family also gathered
for Christmas devotions every Christmas Eve. The
list was endless, and now all of this was gone. In the
daughter's words, she felt like part of a "cut flower
generation."

Is it legitimate to stay together in a marriage for the sake of your children? *Yes.* Should their feelings be considered to the point of changing plans for a divorce? *Yes.* Remember, to file for a divorce can set up a generational pattern in your descendents. Cancel any plans for divorce. You will be glad you did . . . and so will your kids.

7

DENOUNCE THE DECEIVER

I will admit, I was "eavesdropping." I overheard a woman say to another woman, "What caused their divorce?" The other woman responded, "I think it was just the fact that they were incompatible." I mused on that and realized that "incompatibility" is only the façade. The real cause goes much deeper. Why were they incompatible? Personality differences? Temperament differences? Age differences? I believe not.

Marriages are not dissolved for the myriad of reasons given on the surface . . . adultery, finances, in-laws, etc. There is a deeper cause behind them all, and his name is Satan.

By far, most of the couples I have counseled who went ahead and got divorced never realized that they were pawns in the hand of the Devil. Little did they know they were victims of a plot, an orchestrated war, stealthily executed by Satan himself.

In the second chapter of 2 Corinthians, Paul makes a powerful statement about the Devil:

> . . . in order that Satan might not outwit us. For we
> are not unaware of his schemes. (2 Corinthians 2:10b)

The words of Paul suggest to us that Satan has schemes, sinister plans, and designs on us in order to tear us down and to tear down everything that God has called good and sacred.

Have you ever stopped to think why Satan wants all marriages destroyed, especially marriages that are Christian? Let me give you just a few reasons.

1. To Undo God's Original and Most Precious Institution

Think about it. The first institution God ever created was marriage, long before he created the priesthood, the tabernacle, the temple, and the prophetic office. We read about it in the first two chapters of Genesis. God made it clear that in marriage the two would become one flesh, and what He joined together would not be put asunder by man. When you stop and think about it seriously, marriage is the greatest visible testimony to the nature and the love of God. It alone was to be the place where sexual fulfillment was to be realized. It was the place where intimacy was to be fully expressed. Sacred, precious, and of high value, marriage was to be God's showpiece to the world.

If Satan can destroy it, he can mock God before the eyes of an unbelieving world.

Many couples experiencing divorce justify their actions saying, "God doesn't want us unhappy, unfulfilled; and we're better off separate and happy, rather than together and miserable." Guess who planted that demonic idea in their minds? You guessed it, Satan. ". . . for Satan himself masquerades as an angel of light" (2 Corinthians 11:4). Even some of your trusted friends might have been used by Satan as emissaries to convince you that divorce is a better option than staying married and working it out.

2. To Seek to Prove That Forgiveness Does Not Work

Divorce, especially among believers, is a loud and clear announcement to the world that the love and forgiveness taught in Scripture does not really work, is not practical, not "do-able." Since all divorces prove that someone did not forgive, it becomes one of Satan's sharpest weapons to tear down the Christian faith. In an attempt to urge forgiveness on the Ephesian believers, Paul wrote these words:

> In your anger do not sin. Do not let the sun go down while you are still angry, and do not give the Devil a foothold. (Ephesians 4:26–27)

In other words, when refusal to forgive, confirmed by on-going anger, is present, it is proof that you have given Satan a foothold, a hook, an entry way into your life. He does not need a very big opening to put his foot in and bring tyranny into your life. I believe this is one cardinal reason God insisted that marriage be permanent throughout our lives. To end marriage makes a mockery out of all the teaching in Scripture on love, forgiveness, and acceptance. Thus, divorce becomes a signal of victory for the cause of evil.

3. To Cause Other People to Stumble

Satan works on all of us either directly or indirectly through others. That is why the Bible's teaching on human behavior is explicit. "Nobody should seek his own good, but the good of others" (1 Corinthians 10:24).

Again, Paul makes it clear by apostolic command that we need to watch our conduct so that it doesn't cause someone else to fall. "Do not cause anyone to stumble, whether Jews or Greeks, or the church of God" (1 Corinthians 10:31).

As already stated in a previous chapter, the chief people we hurt and cause to stumble are our children. If you have no children, then it is your closest relatives and/or friends.

Satan wants the demise of your marriage, because in so doing, he can pull others down with you. We need to take a firm stand and refuse to allow him to do it. Whether you know it or not, think it or not, someone is watching you. He is watching the decisions you make, the value judgments you render, and the actions you take. Whether you know it or not, someone is building his storehouse of character traits based on what he sees in you. So, when we take God's oldest and most sacred institution, marriage, and cast it aside by divorce, we have given others the license to do the same thing, in spite of the fact that we do not want it that way.

4. To Show the Unbelieving World That There Is Something God Cannot Do

The great testimony of the Christian faith is that God can do anything. Nothing is too hard for God. History bears that out. He parted the Red Sea, miraculously pulled down the walls of Jericho, allowed the Israelites to cross the Jordan on dry ground, and a

> **"Satan wants the demise of your marriage, because in so doing, he can pull others down with you."**

host of other things. Our God is an awesome God, and throughout biblical history, we have seen one power engagement after another between the Lord and the powers of evil. I personally believe that in divorce we see another. Satan comes to steal, kill, and destroy. If he can orchestrate a divorce, it is tantamount to announcing to the world that the salvaging of marriage is one feat God simply cannot pull off, no matter what He has done in the past. Jesus told us about the true nature of the devil.

You belong to your father, the devil, and you want
to carry out your father's desire. He was a mur-
derer from the beginning, not holding the truth, for
there is no truth in him. When he lies, he speaks
his native language, for he is a liar and the father
of lies. (John 8:44)

Satan's deception is strong, most especially in the
area of marriage and divorce. If he can deceive in
marriage, he can deceive just about anywhere. It is
no wonder the book of Revelation says that he "leads
the whole world astray" (Revelation 12:9).

He knows that every marriage which breaks apart
gives more credence to the lie that there is at least
one thing God cannot do, namely, heal a marriage.
That is why he loves to see divorce papers filed. If
the unbelieving world can be shown God's inade-
quacy at any point, Satan knows it will deter them
from surrendering their lives over to Jesus Christ.

5. To Lessen the Authority and Effectiveness Of God's Word

In the parable that Jesus told about the various kinds
of soil and the seed, He made reference to some seed
falling on hard soil, and Satan coming along and taking away that seed: ". . . Satan comes and takes away
the word that was sown" (Mark 4:15).

Satan knows the power of the Word from the
way that Jesus dealt with him using the Word in the
temptations. "It is written . . . ," Jesus said three
times. Satan fled the scene because he cannot stand

up to the power of God's holy Word. So anything Satan can do to lessen God's authority and power, such as break a marriage apart, rest assured he will do it. The Bible quotes God as saying, "I hate divorce" (Malachi 2:16). Every time there is a divorce,

---

"The Word's sharpness and authority is rendered more and more ineffective each time a marriage dissolves."

Satan thinks God's hatred of divorce is lessened and lessened, as perceived in the eyes of the world. The Bible speaks of the "trap of the devil" (2 Timothy 2:26), taking people captive to do his will. Nowhere is this more true than in someone blindly entering the trap of divorce. The credibility of Scripture is chiseled away each time a divorce occurs. The Word's sharpness and authority is rendered more and more ineffective each time a marriage dissolves.

When Peter wrote his first epistle, his target audience was a dispersed people. While they were experiencing perilous and harsh times, he penned these words of warning:

> . . . your enemy the devil prowls around like a roaring lion, looking for someone to devour (1 Peter 5:8).

Before you file for divorce, please know the source of the conflict. Do not settle for a shallow cause.

Finally, learn to denounce the devil. Please realize that the cause of conflict in marriage is not what it is perceived to be, but the root cause is the devil. "Submit yourselves, then, to God. Resist the devil and he will flee from you" (James 4:7).

I have found the following mandate to Satan helpful in helping people face the real culprit in their marriage conflict.

> *Satan, take note and listen well. I command you in Jesus' name to get away from my marriage. I charge you by the power and blood of Jesus to get your hands and influence off of my spouse and me. You have no right to split asunder what God has made one. I come against your influence, your deception, your strategies and your tactics as they pertain to my marriage. I renounce you and your ability to dissolve my marriage. I hereby declare to you today that He that is in me is greater than you who are in the world. You will therefore have no more influence over my marital relationship. In Jesus' name, Amen.*

6. To Destroy a Nation

If you simply follow Satan's logic, you will quickly see how the devil strategizes to destroy a nation, even a civilization.

I have concluded that every "social" problem we face today is really not social at all but at its root is a spiritual problem. Whether the problem is drugs, abortion, immorality, crime, euthanasia, you name it, the root cause usually goes right back to the home. Psychologists call them dysfunctional families, meaning they are not functioning the way families were created to function. But . . . the problem really goes beyond the family. It goes back to the marriage itself that produced the family and is supposed to be in charge of the family.

When a couple decides to end their marriage by means of divorce, they are really aiding and abetting the devil in the destruction of an entire nation and culture. This is why a large majority of men serving time in state and federal penitentiaries come from homes hit by divorce. Many of those convicts have been through two and three sets of parents. Among other things, Satan wants your marriage dissolved so that he can use it as a tool to further destroy our country.

No, incompatibility is not the root cause of the conflict in your marriage, Satan is, and he will not rest until he sees your marriage shredded and destroyed. Denounce him, resist him, and oppose him. Do it now by letting him know that you know he is the *real* culprit. Think about it. Of all the places and events Satan could attack today—the school, the government, the business world, the stock market—none are worth destroying more to him than the home. Satan knows as goes the home in any civilization, so goes the civilization. Rome's fall began when its marriages fell. When you are tempted to end your marriage and file for divorce, remember that when you do, you are playing right into the master plan of the evil one. It is in your hands.

8

COMMUNICATE

In a retreat setting with singles a few years ago, I led a workshop for about thirty or so single men who were divorced. Most were in their thirties and forties. I asked them to list on a sheet of paper in priority what forms of deterioration set in from the time divorce was first discussed in their marriage to the time that the divorce was finalized. I gave them several choices such as sexual relations, money matters, children, etc. Almost to the man, they wrote down, *communication.* It did not surprise me a bit. Communication is usually the first to go, but if acknowledged and corrected, it can avoid a divorce.

Ours is indeed a strange generation. With the dawn of word processors (I'm typing on one now), we are pumping out more words, printing them faster, publishing more books, sending more messages than ever, now on fax machines. Furthermore, many people have a phone in their car because there is no time to stop at a phone booth, to say nothing of the fact that well over 40 percent of homes and 60 percent of all offices now have phone recorders so that we don't miss a word. Yet with all of this modern technology—though we are saying more, doing it faster, and making more copies—we are not communicating as well as we did in the late 1950's! How ironic. This is nowhere more true than in marriage. Most marriages that dissolve do, not because there are not enough words spoken, but because communication does not really take place. It is not the volume of verbiage that counts, but whether we are actually communicating with the words we use. The answer is in most cases, *no.*

I am asking that before you file for divorce, convey to your spouse communication, using the following ground rules.

Avoid Sarcastic And Condemning Words

Some words are like wedges; they drive a chasm between people in a relationship. The old adage, *sticks and stones may break my bones, but words will never hurt me* is a lie out of the pit of hell. Certain words and voice inflections can be cutting and caustic. In checking the word battles going on in Galatia, Paul wrote, "If you keep on biting and devouring each other watch out, or you will be destroyed by each other" (Galatians 5:15). These words of Paul are good advice to husband and wife. Paul tells us more about how our communication ought to be in the following passage: "Let your conversation always be full of grace, seasoned with salt, so that you may know how to answer everyone" (Colossians 4:6).

To that same church Paul sent a message to husbands to love their wives and to not be "harsh" with them (Colossians 3:19).

When divorce is being considered, it is amazing how human decency disappears from marriages. We not only become caustic in our remarks but extremely accusatory. Accusations fly fast and furious. This is rated as highly explosive speech and has no place in a marriage. No real communication can take place in a marriage until we have rooted out every last vestige of accusing and condemning speech.

Speak Truth and Be Transparent

The second thing mentioned in the list of things God hates in the sixth chapter of Proverbs is a "lying tongue." Lying corrodes all trust in marriage. Lying takes many forms:

- Falsifying a report.
- Exaggeration.
- Giving an impression about something we know is not true.
- Hedging when asked a question.
- Truth withheld through silence.

Marriage is built on a mutual trust. When that trust is shattered by untruth or constant exaggerations, there is not much left.

Lying has no regard for those to whom the lie is told. In fact, Solomon said, "A lying tongue hates those it hurts . . ." (Proverbs 26:28).

Avoid Words of Blame

Blaming is a common sin in marriage. Attaching blame on the other spouse removes the spotlight from the "blamer." It is one of the most destructive forms of "un-communication" there is. "It's all your fault; if you hadn't allowed Suzie to go to the party, all this wouldn't have happened." Sound familiar? Some married people have become experts at shifting the blame. This destructive conversation drives a sharp, wide wedge between a relationship quickly.

Before you file for divorce, check this area of your communication and ask yourself these questions.

- Am I quick to blame my spouse for my own problems?

- Do I tend to avoid all responsibility for my own actions?

- Do I feel that accepting blame weakens my position in the marriage?

- Do I feel that admitting blame is a weakness in character?

Avoid Over-Statements

Since much of communication in marriage is *re*-action instead of action, many spouses tend to constantly make over-statements to their spouse. Have you ever heard any of these?

- "You *always* fly off the handle when we discuss things."

- "You *always* spend too much when you go to the store."

- "You *always* pick drab colors when buying a dress."

- "You *always* go into a shell when we have differences."

- "You *always* feel bad or are tired when I want to make love."

- "You overcook the roast every time."

- "You make a royal mess every time you do a project."

Over-statements have a way of putting down our mates and killing off in them any feelings they may have for us. They tend to reduce any meaningful communication coming out of our spouse. Avoid this pitfall at all costs.

When Paul says that our conversation needs to be "full of grace, seasoned with salt" (Colossians 4:6), he means that it needs to be soft and tender, not harsh and critical. Grace in that passage refers to that which has finesse and beauty, that which is soft and lovely. Before you file for divorce, make sure that you "clean up your speech" before it goes into the ears and heart of your spouse.

Learn to Listen

Most of us are very poor listeners because we live in a world saturated with verbiage; and we feel that any silence on our part needs to be used as time to assemble what we are going to say, not a time to listen to what others are saying. This is true in virtually every area of our lives, not just marriage. But it is particularly true in marriage where most of us take communication for granted. Listen to the good advice James gives:

> My dear brothers, take note of this: Everyone should be quick to listen, slow to speak and slow to become angry . . . (James 1:19)

Note, *quick* to listen, *slow* to speak. It is amazing how we have turned those two things around. It's like turning around the statement, "I have a large church and a beautiful wife." That turned around could be dangerous . . . but so can the maxim in James. Someone said that we need to remember that God gave us two ears but only one mouth, meaning we should listen twice as much as we speak. Good advice. Most lack of communication does not come from what is said but from what is never heard.

I have discovered in doing marriage counseling through the years that males have more difficulty communicating than females. Women tend to be "feelers" in their conversation, while men tend to be thinkers only. They may hear the "words" their wives are speaking, but they usually miss the "message" wrapped up in those words. While their wives are talking, men are generally "thinking" how they can respond in such a way so as to protect their male macho image. Thus, they seldom hear the communi-

---

"Most lack of communication does not come from what is said, but from what is never heard."

---

cation of their wives. Solomon said it succinctly: "He who answers before listening—that is his folly and his shame" (Proverbs 18:13).

Remember the Awesome Power Of Your Words

We tend to forget that our words carry with them an awesome power. I have to be reminded often that as a preacher I have an awesome responsibility to preach truth and to do it as tactfully and un-offensively as possible. It tends to make me weigh my words very carefully before I speak. Our words, in a sense, have the power to create and the power to destroy. "The tongue has the power to life and death . . ." (Proverbs 18:21). Our words can justify or condemn us.

But I tell you that men will have to give an account on the day of judgment for every careless word they have spoken. *For by your words you will be acquitted, and by your words you will be condemned.* (Matthew 12:36–37, emphasis added)

What a solemn warning to all of us.

One attorney recently told me that more marriages are broken by the tongue than by the pen used to sign the decree. I think he's probably right. Be careful what you say, and remember that you have the power to utterly destroy a marriage or heal a marriage by your tongue.

The "Ten Commandments" Of Effective Communication

1. *Think Before You Speak.* Weigh your words carefully and have them pass through three gates. Are they true? Are they helpful? Are they necessary?

2. *Never Yell at Your Mate.* Since a *soft* answer turns away wrath, speak in a normal loving tone of voice.

3. *Never Say, "You Always . . ."* It only conveys to your mate that you feel they can never do anything right.

4. *Be Complimentary.* You can always find *something* to compliment your spouse about.

5. *Never Use Derogatory Name-Calling.* It always creates animosity that you are sorry for later.

6. ***Be Truthful About the Way You Really Feel.*** Do not cover up your feelings just to avoid a conflict.

7. ***Never Speak in an Angry Tone of Voice.*** How you speak is as important as what you say.

8. ***Never Lie to Your Spouse.*** Tell the truth even at the risk of being misunderstood.

9. ***Always Find the Time to Communicate.*** It seems like you never *have* the time to talk, so you must *make* the time.

10. ***It Is Never Too Late!*** Even if you have already filed for divorce, it's not too late to re-open the lines of communication. Do it now!

"More marriages are broken by the tongue than by the pen used to sign the decree."

One of the most common communication killers comes in the form of selfishness, wanting things only your way. If you have had difficulty communicating with your spouse, why not try humbling yourself before him or her and saying, "I really want to express myself clearly, and I want you to do the same. If I say anything to offend you, stop me and I will do my best to make it right." That is truly a humble approach to serious communication.

Another communication killer comes in the form pride. "I don't have to take this; I don't have to listen to this; I have a right to better verbal treatment than that . . ." and on the pride goes. Remember, when people are hurt, they do not communicate normally. They say things they really don't mean and often in a tone of voice they really don't want to convey, but that is how it comes out. Take that into consideration when making an attempt to communicate. The price of communication is much less expensive than forging ahead with a divorce. You'll be so glad you paid that price!

It's amazing to discover how little some couples really know about each other. Some men, for example, do not have a clue about what their wife's favorite color, fruit, movie, magazine, or restaurant happens to be. Many wives, if quizzed, could not come up with what their husband's favorite sport or vacation spot happens to be. Time must be carved out in your marriage for conversation. It may be done on long walks, over lunches, listening to music, but it must be done. Television has become a communication blocker, especially in the fall when Monday night football is on. It has to be the time of the lowest level of communication in marriages in the country. Along with television, over-crowded schedules have contibuted to the communication breakdown in our marriages. Somewhere between little league, scouts, ballet lessons, garden club, bowling, and jobs, couples are expected to communicate. Whatever it takes, however long it takes, *communicate!* And when you do, be clear, be kind, be tender, and be consistent. Solomon was right when he said:

> A word aptly spoken is like apples of gold in a setting of silver. (Proverbs 25:11)

9

CALCULATE THE CONSEQUENCES

S omeone once said, *"Too many marry for better or for worse, but not for good."* In a culture where nearly sixty-five out of every one hundred marriages end in divorce, the consequences must be considered. Much is written and filmed about the pros and cons of divorce. Much is said on talk shows about causes of divorce. Many are the books dealing with the ethics of divorce and how much it costs in money and time, but I have read and seen little dealing with the *consequences* of divorce. I recently saw a large billboard with a picture of a totally wrecked automobile. The caption at the top of the picture read: *If you drink and drive, be prepared to live with your choices.* It is true, is it not, that we live in the kind of world where we must live with our choices. Those who smoke all their lives are likely to live and die with emphysema. Those who do drugs are likely to have permanent brain damage to one degree or another. Those who are sexually promiscuous may have to live with the consequence of venereal diseases including AIDS. People who waltz through life with loose spending habits and with no financial discipline will someday live with the consequences of poverty and debt. We live with our choices!

If you have ever contemplated divorce, or entertained any thoughts about the possibility of divorce, please calculate the consequences before you file.

What are those consequences? Here are a few you might want to weigh.

Severe Economic Impact

Married couples encounter many big ticket items in the course of their marriage: down payments for homes, new cars, washers, dryers, boats, etc. But none are as devastating as the economics involved in a divorce. Even with "divorce kits" now available in bookstores, the process of divorce is a big ticket item.

I recently asked an attorney friend if he could give me a ballpark figure of the cost of a divorce. His response was shocking to me, to say the least. I was not prepared for his matter-of-fact calculation. He said that today, the average divorce will cost a couple half the price of a new import luxury car. Since these cars presently sell for thirty to forty thousand dollars, I asked him if he was talking about a figure of around sixteen or seventeen thousand dollars on the average. His response? "If they're lucky and don't get involved in an intense property settlement dispute. And that's just the process and the dissolution." In my attorney's words, there are always four people legally involved in a divorce suite: the husband's attorney, the wife's attorney, the husband,

and the wife. Only two people ever really win and gain something. That's right, it's the two lawyers!

Now don't blame the lawyers, they did not go to the couple with legal advice. The couple sought the counsel of their respective attorneys. The cost of obtaining the divorce is only the beginning.

Tom sat across from me and said:

> Pastor, I don't know what I'm going to do. The court has just decreed that my child support and maintenance payments be increased to $275 monthly. My take-home pay is only $1780 monthly after taxes and the credit union deduction. My rent is $525 monthly, though I'm looking for a roommate. My utilities are $135 each month from my apartment. My food (I'm eating very little) is about $250 a month. Car insurance is now over $100 monthly, and I'm paying on some medical bills at the clip of $100 monthly. On top of all that, I'm trying to pay my parents back on a $2000 loan.

Well, it did not take me long to see that Tom was in financial trouble, all brought on by the fact that he opted to file for divorce. He was going to have to radically lower his standard of living for the luxury of terminating his marriage. Was the divorce worth it? Hardly. But he was living with his choice.

On the other hand, Pam poured her heart out to me in desperation. She was in her fourth month as a single parent of three children. The $175 a month child support per child as arranged by the court had only been paid one month, the first month, and only a portion of it paid the second month. None was paid the third and fourth month. Her husband was laid off his job, and what she had counted on to survive was not coming in. Because she had never worked as a married woman outside the home, she began a job at entry level pay. She was about four hundred dollars short of making it every month. I have never seen such a stressful look on someone's face.

Divorced people end up paying more for about everything and seem to never have enough to get by. In some cases it is tantamount to paying the bills on two households instead of one on the same income.

By far most of the people who seek financial help from our church are divorced people who simply aren't making it. Please, before you file for divorce, calculate the economic hardship it brings.

Divorce Creates
An "Unprotected Species"

From a biblical perspective, most couples do not consider that one of the most disastrous consequences of divorce is the creation of an unprotected species, namely the woman. The Bible teaches that in marriage, the husband becomes the umbrella of protection over the wife. He is called the head of the marriage, not just because he is the God-ordained authority in the institution, but because he is also the insulation of protection God has provided for the woman.

> Now I want you to realize that the head of every
> man is Christ, and the head of the woman is man,
> and the head of Christ is God. (1 Corinthians 11:3)

That is God's pecking order. So, when a woman's covering is removed by means of divorce, she becomes unprotected and uncovered and becomes a sitting duck to all kinds of predators. Divorced women often experience all kinds of harassment once their covering is removed. They are often taken advantage of by repair people; they are sexually harassed on the job; and they are seen as easy prey by unscrupulous sales people. How sad . . . but unfortunately, true.

I can think of no worse consequence of divorce. Whatever the differences you're encountering with your spouse, please ask yourself, "Is this worse than the alternative, the removal of protection from the woman?"

An On-Going Affected Conscience

Like any other sin we commit, a biblically unjustified divorce pricks one's conscience. No matter how badly one desires to get out of a marriage, deep down, there is a twinge of conscience, if the truth is known. Fortunately, divorce is forgiveable, like other sins, but the scars remain in a different way. Though forgiven, because of the emotional part of our make-up, the spouse who initiated the divorce, or the one who refused to try to stop it, has an on-going guilt that tends to affect and pervade every other area of life.

One man whose marriage ended after twenty-one years confided in me recently that when he left the marriage, his motto was "out of sight out of mind." He wanted nothing to do with his wife, ever again. He had found new interests in life. But eighteen months after his divorce was final, he said, "When does the guilt go away?" I am not sure it will in his case until appropriate restitution is made, namely the reestablishment of his marriage covenant with his wife. As long as your divorced spouse is alive, some of the guilt will remain. Before you file for divorce, make sure you know that the deep-seated guilt is likely to stay with you for years to come. Yes, divorce is forgiveable, but the scars remain, and they hurt for a long time.

A Damaged Testimony

Of course, when any believer sins, it damages his testimony before the eyes of both the believing and the unbelieving world. But when one divorces, that testimony is damaged more deeply because in the eyes of many, right or wrong, divorce is an on-going sin, since the divorcees continue to live. If statisticians are correct, there are as many divorces among Christian people as there are among non-Christian people. That being true, it makes for a bad testimony for both the initiator of the divorce and the spouse who did not initiate it. It sends a message to weak and strong that it really does not make any difference whether you are a Christian or not, divorce is going

---

"Yes, divorce is forgiveable, but the scars remain, and they hurt for a long time."

---

to occur. We need to change that perception; and for a Christian, if there was no other reason to stay married, this reason should be paramount.

A Lowered View
Of God's Unlimited Ability

Christians put their faith for salvation in a God who is merciful, faithful, and extremely powerful. We preach that there is nothing God cannot do. We quote the passage from Ephesians to support this belief:

> Now to him who is able to do immeasurably more than all we ask or imagine, according to his power that is at work within us, to him be glory in the church, and in Christ Jesus throughout all generations, for ever and ever. (Ephesians 3:20–21)

A divorce is tantamount to admitting to the world that God can indeed do anything, that is, almost anything. The only thing He cannot do is keep a marriage together! Divorce is an admission that in this department, God is not omnipotent. It is a confession that in "my case" God did not prove to be all powerful; that there was a defect, a flaw in His omnipotent nature. Of course, we all know that God has

no flaws, but a divorce sends the message to the unbelieving world that at this point God failed. He
didn't prove Himself totally able and faithful. I believe this is a significant consequence. The Bible
makes it clear that we are to live so as not to make
others stumble by what we eat, drink, say, or do. In
an area so insignificant as eating meat, Paul says:
"Therefore if what I eat causes my brother to fall into
sin, I will never eat meat again so I will not cause
him to fall" (1 Corinthians 8:13). Again, he says, "Do
not cause anyone to stumble, whether Jews or Greeks
or the church of God" (1 Corinthians 10:32).

When a believer files for divorce, he causes someone to stumble, someone to think less of Christianity,
someone to put off becoming a Christian, someone to
readjust his own standards downward. Every time
there is a divorce, it casts aspersions on God's power.

Divorce Encourages a Precedent
For a Divorce Pattern in Offspring

As already mentioned, the chances of your children
divorcing are greatly increased if you divorce. It is
somehow a generational thing. More than 50 percent
of all divorces filed for today are filed for by couples
where either the husband, the wife, or both have parents who were divorced. The majority of divorces
today occur in situations where one of the spouse's
parents are divorced. Yes, I am aware that there are
many people whose parents are divorced, but they
aren't. However, that does not eliminate the fact that

a pattern is usually set which is followed by the off-spring. I would think that as a parent, we would not want to do anything that would cause our children, or even provide a model for our children, to divorce.

Divorce Increases the Tendency For a Pattern of Failure

In my own counseling room, I have discovered over a period of years that those who fail in their marriage tend, in many cases, to fail in other areas of their lives. They tend to fail in their careers, in other relationships, in finances, health, and noble endeavors they may attempt.

This is not to say that if you get a divorce your future is doomed to failure, but it is to say that a tendency is definitely there.

I believe there is a good reason for this. Marriage is the oldest and most sacred institution God ever created. It was to be held in awe. There is no relationship in life (apart from our relationship to Jesus Christ), that is more intimate and more personal than marriage. It has a way of pervading every area of our life. If we fail in the most basic and important relationship, it is not as likely that we will succeed in less important relationships with relatives and friends, or in our jobs, financial responsibilities, etc. A man in his mid-forties confided in me that since his divorce, which occurred in his mid-thirties, he has had great difficulty in holding a job, setting and fulfilling goals, and staying at his proper weight. In his own words,

"It seems like from the day I left my wife, every other area in my life degenerated." His testimony is not an isolated one. That tendency is definitely there. It is almost as if God is saying to us, "If you can't succeed in life's most primary and significant institution, you probably won't succeed in the lesser areas of your life either."

Divorce Increases the Chances Of Entering into an Unbiblical Marriage

Studies disclose that people who divorce are very likely to remarry. In fact, men usually marry much more quickly than women. The second marriage, however, is not all roses. The thorns are all too present. Because of loneliness, people tend to marry too quickly, often entering into a marriage before they are healed from the dissolution of their first marriage; and the tendency is either to marry a non-Christian or to simply remarry when, biblically speaking, one member of the couple is not eligible. The Bible teaches that unless the reason for your divorce was adultery or abandonment by an unbelieving partner, you are not biblically eligible to remarry. Supposing that your divorce is one allowed by Scripture, to remarry while your first spouse is alive and unmarried is often to invite disaster. Tragically, second marriages do not have the survival rate that first marriages have. There are many reasons for that, but the general reason is that God never intended us to be in and out of several marriages. Of course, if your spouse dies, you are free to remarry in the Lord. But to turn around and remarry after going through a biblically unjustified divorce is a move that most

---

> ### "If you can't succeed in life's most primary and significant institution, you probably won't succeed in the lesser areas of your life either."

---

people live to regret. Furthermore, if you remarry after being divorced for a reason that *is* biblically sound, the adjustment is still very, very difficult; and in more than 50 percent of the cases that marriage also fails.

Loneliness That Can Result in Sin

Only those who have been through it can really tell the story. Carl sat across from my desk, a broken man. His wife had divorced him two years ago, in spite of his heroic attempts to fight the divorce. He lost. He had moved into a one-bedroom apartment where he pined away from loneliness. He would go to work, come home to a quiet, cold, empty apartment, turn on the television, and stay with it until he fell asleep. In his words, he was living a horrible life. He was dying inside with loneliness. He met Edna in the laundry room one Saturday. They made popcorn together, went to movies, and took walks. What he thought was nothing more than a friendship for two lonely people turned into something he would live to regret all his life. One night in her apartment, Carl gave in to his sexual drive and stayed all night. He felt dirty, ashamed, embarrassed, and angry at himself. He told his teenaged children because he could not get his conscience cleared. While they were understanding, Carl was not only devastated by a divorce, but by the fact that he had sex for the first time in his life outside of marriage.

Divorce brings loneliness and often our own family cannot seem to fill that void, so the temptation is always there, ready to drag us down if we allow.

Carl is not just a lone exception. Many fall into the trap in which he found himself. It is one of the consequences that can result from the loneliness that always invades when one is divorced.

It is true, we live with our choices. When those choices are out of the will of God, though we can and will be forgiven upon repentance, the scars remain. Before you file for divorce, please calculate the consequences. They are not pleasant, fun, or easy. Many of the consequences will not just go away if we ignore them, either.

No, it is not easy working through your differences. No, it won't always be done with one or two or even three tries; but knowing the consequences, we need to try very hard and realize that virtually no divorce is worth the consequences that follow. Maybe you're wondering, "What if I'm the victim in a divorce that I didn't want? Do I have to endure all those consequences?"

I truly believe that God protects His own. Sin always brings bad consequences, whether it is our sin or someone else's. To say you will not reap some of the consequences would not be honest. But there is a good passage for you if you are the victim of a divorce you did not want:

> And my God will meet all your needs according to his glorious riches in Christ Jesus. (Philippians 4:19)

Claim that promise; it's for you!

10

WATCH THE WARNINGS

I bought my wife a good, clean used car. It had all the whistles and bells on it. But to our utter surprise, it had another feature that caught us off guard. We were driving along the freeway, and out of the blue, in stereophonic sound, a voice interrupted the radio and said with authority, *"Your fuel is low!"* It was like a little man in our dash board that was giving us fair warning. Later, we found that same little man had other verses to his computerized advice: *"A door is ajar"; "Please fasten your seatbelt"; "Your windshield washer fluid is low."* On and on the warnings go, and I am sure we have not heard all of them yet! I keep wondering if the voice is going to name our sins, tell us to repent, or warn us of traffic ahead so that we can take the appropriate exit.

As I hear his voice from time to time, I have thought . . . Wouldn't it be wonderful in a marriage if technology could build a warning voice that could speak with some kind of authority, alerting us to those danger areas we seem to blindly enter with no warning. While we will have to wait for technology to produce such a device, I can tell you there are some warning signals that are screaming at us if only we have ears to hear. Nobody wakes up some morning and says, "Oh, I think I'll file for divorce today." No, that decision is mostly made after weeks, months, and maybe even years of built-up animosity, resentment, distrust, suspicion, and non-communication.

Long before you file for divorce, please observe these warning signs. I was waiting in a doctor's office recently, and noticed a sign on the wall urging men over fifty to be checked for prostate cancer. In bold red letters at the bottom of the sign were these words:

Remember . . . early detection can avoid early death!

These are timely words for men and their prostates, and for couples in marriage. I am convinced that Satan is convinced that the best way to discredit God's Kingdom is to devastate marriages, namely Christian marriages. He is fairly successful at the moment since various surveys indicate that divorce among Christian couples ranks as high as divorce among non-Christian couples. Therefore, we had better know the warning signals that subtly eat away at our marriages; yet, we do not even know the marriage is crumbling until it is too late.

While these warning signals are in no particular order of importance, I begin with what is perhaps the most subtle.

Boredom

I will call them Sandy and Terry. When I heard they had separated, I called Terry to find out what was going on. By the way, many divorces could be cancelled if Christian friends would confront their

---

"I am convinced that Satan is convinced that the best way to discredit God's Kingdom is to devastate marriages, namely Christian marriages."

---

friends when they hear of trouble. Accountability and concern are of utmost importance. Otherwise, divorce-bound couples begin to think that nobody really cares.

Terry's words were words I had heard dozens of times before. "There's no fun in my marriage anymore. It's all so boring. She says the same things, wears the same clothes, prepares the same meals on the same day . . . there's no flare anymore." In talking with Sandy, she said practically the same thing about Terry. They had a case of the "boredom blahs." It's called "marriage-in-a-rut." Don't get me wrong. There is a routineness about life, work, marriage, etc., that is healthy and frankly unavoidable. We must eat, sleep, work, shower, brush teeth; these things are routine. But other things don't have to be. Terry disclosed to me frankly, "We eat spaghetti on Monday, watch these shows on Tuesday evening, have sex on Tuesdays, Thursdays, and Fridays, go to her mother's on Wednesday for dinner, balance the checkbook on Saturday morning, and start the whole process over again."

While some things must be routine, let me encourage all of you to "switch days, switch meals, switch places you sit, the side of the bed on which you sleep, the days on which you go places, etc." Be spontaneous on occasions, do the unexpected, go to new places, meet new friends. When people tell me they are splitting up because they are bored with each other, I remind them that boredom is something they can remedy. Someone said, "A successful marriage is like falling in love often . . . with the same person." How true, how true!

Independence

This warning signal of the need for independence is difficult to spot and identify because it is usually verbalized as: "I need my space, I have my rights, I'm still an individual person, etc." In the marriage ceremony, we quote the Scripture, "the two shall become one, . . ." but *which* one?

Every divorce (without exception) that I have ever witnessed began somewhere with a spirit of independence, detachment, a "do-your-own-thing" mentality. The scenario begins like this. The husband and wife get so wrapped up in doing their own "thing" that they lose interest in each other. For the male, it's often his work. He becomes a workaholic; and the wife reacts by picking up a hobby, an interest, or a job outside the home. He then, sensing her independence, becomes more independent himself. Along the way, one of them meets prince or princess charming who shows them some individual attention, and bang! It's the beginning of the end.

Here is a plea. Whatever activity, job, hobby, or events in which you are involved that are drawing you away from your spouse instead of closer, drop it like a hot potato. Marriage by its essence is a together thing. No, this does not mean that absolutely *everything* you do must be done with your spouse, but make sure that whatever you are involved in without him or her is sanctioned by your spouse, and that it is not pulling you apart.

My experience has been that husbands are more prone to pull away, affirm independence, do their own thing, than the wife. It may be hunting, fishing, golf, racing, sports, or his job. Men, remember, God is holding you responsible for the success of your marriage since you are the covering and high priest of that merger. An old preacher in the Ozarks gave this piece of timely wisdom for men: *"Troubles in marriage often start when a man is so busy earning his salt that he forgets his sugar."* This is not a deeply profound or intellectual statement, but it sure is true.

I am convinced that if couples will "take charge" early on in their marriages, staying on alert about this subtle danger of the need for independence, they will be able to catch it and deal with it in its infant stages.

Romance Gone Stale

A couple I know who began to take each other for granted, and thus lost much of their romantic affection for each other, shared this statement with me after they woke up and turned things around: "Pastor, if somehow couples could *bottle* the emotional and physical romance of the first three months of marriage, then draw from it for the next fifty years, they would never dream of divorce." Well, there is a way you can "bottle" such romance; keep it fresh, keep it on the front burner. Peter gave a strong piece of advice to husbands: "Husbands, be considerate as you *live* with your wives . . ." (1 Peter 3:7, emphasis added).

The word "live" is an interesting word. It doesn't just mean that a husband has the same address as his wife, or the fact that they live in the same house together. More importantly, "live" means that an appropriate deep emotional relationship exists between the husband and the wife, and this relationship includes the sexual union. In other words, make sure, men, that you experience a closeness with your wife, not only in physical sexual relations, but let an emotional closeness exist between the two of you in the same way as when you are together physically. In short, keep the romance alive by staying close. This requires communication, attention, focusing, sensitivity, and a willingness on the man's part to understand his wife's world, her feelings, and her concerns.

Romance does not have to fly out the window after a few months of marriage. If you feel it's flown out the window in your marriage, get it back. It's recoverable! It has been said, *The bonds of matrimony are a good investment when the interest is kept up.*

Remember men, the command to "love" in marriage was given to the male, not the female. Of course, a wife is to love her husband, but her love is to be the reflection of his love. The command is not, "wives, love your husbands so they will love you," but "husbands, love your wives, . . ." and a loved wife will respond in love.

Non-Communication

Much has been spoken and written about communication in marriage, but apparently not enough! It is a prime killer of marriages. Many couples learn early in marriage what words "set off" their spouse, so they begin to avoid those words. That's followed by avoiding other words. I believe the standing rule of any marriage is that a spouse ought to be able to talk about *anything* to his or her spouse without being threatened. Lack of communication always starts with fear, fear of how the other spouse will react. If it's worth thinking about, it's worth talking about.

There are some areas of conversation we need to avoid in communication. We need to avoid anger, constant criticism, complaining, put-downs, accusations, and arguments. The topic of conversation should not cause you to hesitate. Some couples find it hard to talk about sex, what pleases them, and what bugs them; so they stuff it and keep the other partner guessing. Some spouses fear talking about money because they think it will make their spouse angry.

Here is another plea. *Communicate, Communicate, Communicate.* Most couples who communicate well never divorce. One woman told me after a bitter divorce, "It wasn't what he said, it's what he never said, what he never communicated to me. I never knew what he was thinking, or what he thought of the way I thought. He just clammed up." How tragic. In that case, divorce could have been avoided altogether had the lines of communication been wide open.

Leaving God Out

This subtle sin often happens, and because nobody takes charge, deterioration sets in. It begins with neglecting prayer at mealtime. It then moves on to no prayer time together as a couple; that progresses (or regresses) to no discussion of the spiritual altogether. Church attendance becomes hit and miss, and the focus with which the marriage began soon becomes blurred.

I believe a good verse for every married couple to keep over their marriage is this:

> But seek first his kingdom and his righteousness, and all these things will be given to you as well. (Matthew 6:33)

Does your spouse know that you love Jesus Christ above all else? Do your children know that Christ really comes first in your life? Is it evident in your living, your giving, your speech, your conduct? Without the spiritual aspect of marriage, all the rest falls apart.

"I believe the standing rule of any marriage is that a spouse ought to be able to talk about *anything* to his or her spouse, without being threatened."

Before you think about divorce, much less file for divorce, watch the warnings! Be alert! Cultivate your marriage daily, and you will not even have the word "divorce" in your vocabulary. Our church has a support group, "Healing Wounded Marriages." Every Monday evening almost one hundred individuals come to that meeting. They are a rare breed as people go in our society. In spite of all the advice they receive from neighbors, colleagues, friends and relatives, they have made a decision to "stand" for the healing of their marriage. They refuse to look at outward circumstances, consider marriage an unbreakable covenant; and in spite of the "odds" stacked against the survival of their marriage, they stand with God, and pray. They are spiritually "tough" minded, and determined. Their stand is often costly, painful, lonely, and difficult, but they stand. Once in awhile, if you attend the meetings, you'll hear how someone's marriage was healed. They all applaud, and pray that the next testimony will be theirs. In the back of most of their Bibles is what we call a Stander's Prayer, which they often pray. Is your marriage in trouble now? Why not pray *The Stander's Affirmation?*

> *I am standing for the healing of my marriage! I won't give up, give in, give out or give over till that healing takes place. I made a vow, I said the words, I gave the pledge, I gave a ring, I took a ring, I gave myself, I trusted God, and said the words, and meant the words . . . in sickness and in health, in sorrow and in joy, for better or for worse, for richer or for poorer, in good times and in bad, so I'm standing now, and won't sit down, let down, slow down, calm down, fall down, look down, or be down till the breakdown is torn down!*
>
> *I refuse to put my eyes on outward circumstances, or listen to prophets of doom, or buy into what's trendy, worldly, popular, convenient, easy, quick, thrifty, or advantageous . . . nor will I settle for a cheap imitation of God's real thing, nor will I seek to lower God's standard, twist God's will, rewrite God's Word, violate God's covenant, or accept what God hates, namely divorce.*
>
> *In a world of filth, I will stay pure, surrounded by lies, I will speak the truth, where hopelessness abounds, I will hope in God, where revenge is easier, I will bless instead of curse, and where the odds are stacked against me, I'll trust in God's faithfulness.*
>
> *I'm a stander, and I won't acquiesce, compromise, quarrel or quit . . . I have made the choice,*

*set my face, entered the race, believed the Word,
and trusted God for all the outcome.*

*I will allow neither the reaction of my spouse, nor
the urging of my friends, nor the advice of my loved
ones, nor the economic hardship, nor the prompting
of the devil to make me let up, slow up, blow up, or
give up till my marriage is healed up. Amen.*

I challenge you to pray that prayer. Be a stander,
and be resolved to stand for the healing of your marriage. Remember, as we have already said, marriage
is a three-way covenant between you, your spouse,
and God. It only takes a simple majority to stand,
you and God. Do it! Ten years from now, you'll be
glad you did.

11

DIVORCE-PROOF YOUR MARRIAGE

I saw it in Daytona Beach, Florida with my own eyes. Across the street from where we were staying, they had covered an entire house with a large canvas cover so that you couldn't even see any of the house. It looked like a large paper bag had been placed over the house. As I walked over to see what was going on, I saw the sign of a local exterminating company. The worker told me that's how they do it in Florida, and after releasing the deadly fumes for twenty-four hours, every ant, roach, termite, or anything else that crawls would be dead. The company guaranteed that house to be free from bugs for at least two years.

I thought as I saw the process . . . Wouldn't it be wonderful if you could take such a canvas on a smaller scale, cover a couple with it, and exterminate their marriage until it is divorce-proof. With almost one half of all first time marriages ending in divorce within the first seven years, such a "divorce exterminator" could become a wealthy person.

I was recently told that the average cost of a wedding in the upper northeast region of our country runs as high as eighteen thousand dollars, while many run as high as twenty-four thousand dollars! Isn't it amazing that people will spend that kind of money to get married in a ceremony that averages nineteen minutes, but will not spend the time and energy it takes to stay married over a lifetime.

Today is the day of prenuptial agreements. I am told that nearly one half of all second marriages begin with a legal prenuptial agreement, most of which have to do with money. Such agreements are also on the rise in first-time marriages. Such a trend speaks of the fragile nature of modern marriages. In none of these agreements are words like commitment, devotion, fidelity, or loyalty mentioned. In all of them, terms like "in case of" or "in the event of" are common. Most of them are designed to protect the spouses from a financial wipe-out. How tragic.

What would happen if a "divorce-proof" prenuptial agreement were entered upon that sounded like this?

> We, the undersigned, being of legal age and of sound mind, do hereby enter into a binding agreement that our marriage to each other will be until death. In the event of a divorce, God forbid, each of us agrees to turn over everything we own to the other partner, down to the last dime we have in our pocket, and both agree that we will never marry anyone else ever again in our lifetime.

Unheard of? Maybe, but the thought intrigues me. I believe you can divorce-proof your marriage, using a combination of common sense and the Word of God.

Agree Now To Hate
Divorce As God Does

In His teaching on marriage, Jesus made it abundantly clear that though Moses allowed a man to write a certificate of divorce, it was not in the mind of God in the beginning (Matthew 19:8). In fact, He went on to say that it was because of hardness of heart that divorce was even permitted. In other words, the concession came from the hardness of man's heart, not from the will of God's heart. If you want God's assessment of divorce, listen to Him. "'I hate divorce,' says the Lord God of Israel . . ." (Malachi 2:16).

In a sense, all divorce is a compromise of the will of God. Far from God's best, it is calculated to be man's worst. Apart from the consequences, which in themselves are miserable, divorce is a perversion of God's best for our lives. We are told in Scripture to "hate what is evil; cling to what is good" (Romans 12:9b). Since divorce is evil, and since God hates it, we need to train ourselves to hate even the mention of it. I know a couple who on their wedding night made a vow to God and to each other that they would never speak that word audibly in the presence of the other. They have now been married almost three years, and their vow is still intact.

Make Commitment, Not Feeling
The Basis of Your Marriage

We live in the era of "feelings" and moods. *If it feels good, do it,* we are told today. Life-long decisions are made on the basis of feeling, not fact. The kind of love required to make a marriage last will not rely on feelings each day, but on the fact that each spouse is committed to the other for the long haul. Feelings come and go. They are altered by circumstances. When the bills are paid, we feel good. When there is too much month left over at the end of the money, however, we become terse, fitful, critical, and judgmental. When we are in good health, we have no problem expressing romantic love to our spouse. But let a headache persist, and an upset stomach prevail, or pain in any other way come upon us, and our "love" is affected. Divorce can never be considered, however, if your love for your spouse is based on a commitment you have to him/her, a commitment to fidelity, trust, and staying together, no matter what. In ancient times a law prevailed in parts of Egypt that forbade divorce under any circumstances. Violators were hanged in the city square without a trial! Guess what the divorce rate was under that law? Zero! It's amazing how couples worked out their problems when the alternative was death! I concede that we would flinch under such a prohibition today, but maybe it's a lesser of the other evil that prevails, that is, divorce at the drop of a hat.

Commitment in marriage does not just mean that we promise to have sex with no one but our spouse. It is also a pledge that no matter what circumstance rears its ugly head, you will not bail out.

My wife and I sat outside to watch a Hawaiian singing group near the beach in Waikiki. They concluded their little concert under the stars by singing

the Hawaiian Wedding Song. They invited those cel-
ebrating their anniversary to come up and dance.
One couple went up and danced who had been married fifty-seven years. I watched them as they moved
very slowly, bent with age, but they danced, and

"Divorce can never be considered . . . if your love for your spouse is based on a commitment . . . to fidelity, trust, and staying together, no matter what."

---

held each other in their arms. Was life always so
smooth? Hardly. I'm sure there were plenty of times
when they thought of "bailing out" because the
going was rough, but it was commitment that kept
them together, even in times when "romance"
seemed thin or altogether missing. Commitment is
the key.

Learn to Draw a Very Large Circle of Love

When I used to counsel couples prior to marriage, I
would share with them a little poem that was shared
with me many years ago:

> *He drew a circle that shut me out,*
> *Heretic, rebel, a thing to flout,*

But love and I had the wit to win,
We drew a circle that took him in.

I like that poem because it shows me how I need never act outside the circle of love. It's really very simple if we will but remember. When our spouse does or says something that our love circle cannot accept or tolerate, draw a larger circle instead of rigidly holding on to the circumference of the circle you have. I believe that the words of Jesus, "If you love those who love you, what reward will you get?" (Matthew 5:46) apply to marriage as well as our other relationships. In other words, it is easy to love our spouse as long as he/she operates within the circle of love I have drawn for him/her. But when our spouse steps outside that circle, *watch out!* No, if you want to divorce-proof your marriage, you will keep your "love pencil" handy and draw larger circles throughout your marriage. Larger circles prevent friction, confrontation, and guarding your turf. And guess what? When you draw that larger circle, your spouse will often reverse the behavior that demanded the larger circle and so behave to get back into the previous smaller circle. The game is even more exciting when *both* partners play! You have probably guessed the secret of this by now. There will always be a surplus of love when you are flexible with your love.

Practice Positive Words, Not Negative Words in Conversation

The power of the tongue is far greater than most people know. The Bible says that with it we bless, and with it we curse (James 3:9). Though every animal has been tamed, no human can tame the tongue (James 3:8). It is a restless evil, full of deadly poison (James 3:8b). In fact, remember the Scripture we shared earlier? "The tongue has the power of life and death . . ." (Proverbs 18:21). We truly underestimate the power of the tongue. Destructive words have assassinated more marriages than man can count. If you want to divorce-proof your marriage, you will be well on your way by deciding and determining to speak only upbuilding words to your mate. Avoid terms like: "You always; You never; I can't believe you're so dumb; Well, you did it again, etc." Learn to compliment, affirm, endorse, and encourage your mate. This can only come about by speaking positive words. The best advice that can be heeded are the words of Scripture:

> Do not let unwholesome talk come out of your mouths, but only what is helpful for building others up according to their needs, that it may benefit those who listen. (Ephesians 4:29)

Never Go to Bed at Night Angry With Each Other

Keep short accounts! Paul knew what he was talking about in Ephesians:

> In your anger do not sin. Do not let the sun go down while you are still angry, and do not give the devil a foothold. (Ephesians 4:26–27)

In some of the older versions, it says, "be angry." In other words, the Bible acknowledges that times of anger will come. They come at work, at play, and in marriage. The point is not whether or not anger will come, but how we will handle it. The injunction is clear: "Do not let the sun go down while you are still angry." Truer words were never spoken. What we go to bed with, we usually awaken with, except it becomes more ingrained in us. Clear the slate before retiring, even if it means you must "swallow crow" and humble yourself. It's worth it. Furthermore, if you have trouble forgiving your spouse, just remember all for which Christ has forgiven you (Ephesians 4:32).

Pray Together Regularly

Even among believers, very few married couples pray together. There is great power in united prayer. Some of the closest times my wife and I have with each other are when we are holding hands and praying together. It is amazing how differences and incompatibilities fade when you are in that position. Jesus gave us a revolutionary truth about prayer: "Again, I tell you that if two of you on earth agree about anything you ask for, it will be done for you by my father in heaven" (Matthew 18:19). Though not confined to married couples, I believe that text works well for married couples. It tells me that if I agree with my wife and she agrees with me, we can agree together in prayer, and God will answer. What greater place of need than in marriage for prayer to work?

Determine That You Will
Never Start an Argument

Solomon was right: "Starting a quarrel is like breaching a dam; so drop the matter before a dispute breaks out" (Proverbs 17:14).

Have you ever stopped to think about what causes an argument between spouses? Words! Guess what prevents an argument from breaking out? You guessed it right, the absence of words! Drop the matter before it becomes a "supreme court" issue. One man told me that his wife had become an expert in starting an argument, but he had become a better ex-

---

"If you have trouble forgiving your spouse, just remember all for which Christ has forgiven you."

---

pert in stopping it. He simply would not respond negatively to her barrage of words, and this took all the "fun" out of her attempted argument. After about a year of this, they had no more arguments because he simply kept his mouth shut. It really takes two people to keep an argument going.

I have discovered that arguments are destructive in marriage for both partners. If each of you will make a concerted attempt to never be the one to start an argument, guess what? You will have an argument-free marriage.

ᘔ　ᘔ　ᘔ

I can honestly say that I have never talked to a divorced person who did not have some great regrets that he/she followed through with the divorce. Let me urge you, especially if you are even thinking about divorce, to make the following your declaration.

> *I rebuke, in Jesus' name, the spirit of divorce. I confess that it is not of God, not wholesome, not right, and against God's Holy Word. I stand on the premise of God's inerrant Word that "all things are possible to him who believes." I hereby acknowledge my belief in the power of God for a whole marriage for my spouse and me. I hereby place my marriage in His hands, and renounce all attempts by Satan to destroy my marriage, thereby destroying my witness and testimony. I concur with God, "I hate divorce." I will do all within my power and God's to make my marriage all it was intended to be.*

Like the tent that covered the house in Florida for extermination, you also can cover your marriage and make it "divorce-proof." Are you willing?

12

BUT WHAT IF?

I f you have managed to "hang on" this far, you are probably thinking, "But he doesn't know *my* situation." Over the years, I have had both men and women say to me, "If anybody had grounds for divorce, I certainly do," and then they would proceed to tell me bizarre aberrations about their spouse. This chapter is not meant to be an exhaustive listing of all the exceptions, different situations, and special cases in marriage; but perhaps as you read this, you can identify.

But What If My Spouse
Has Committed Adultery?

Almost every month a new statistic appears in the newspaper or a magazine concerning the rising practice of infidelity in marriages. Some of these say that as many as 50 percent of all married men commit adultery at least once in their married life. I am suspicious about statistics, but I would not be surprised at the accuracy of that one.

There has been much confusion over what the Bible teaches concerning the innocent party's "rights" in an adultery situation. What does the Bible really say? Jesus says:

> I tell you that anyone who divorces his wife, except for marital unfaithfulness, and marries another woman, commits adultery. (Matthew 19:9)

First, let us clear the air on one thing. Jesus does not say here that anyone has a responsibility to divorce his or her spouse because they have been sexually unfaithful. So we are not commanded to automatically divorce because our spouse has been unfaithful. The point of his statement is that if you divorce your wife, you commit adultery. The exception clause is not the main point of the sentence; it is only the exception clause. Jesus is saying that you *may* divorce your spouse in the case of adultery, but you certainly do not have to. In fact, in the light of other Scripture, your obligation to forgive takes precedence over your *right* to divorce. In fact, the only time you have a right to withhold forgiveness is if you have not sinned yourself (Ephesians 4:32).

Therefore, if your spouse has shattered your trust by being sexually unfaithful, and he or she has repented and requested your forgiveness, as a Christian, you have an obligation to forgive him/her. If that spouse *continues* in the sin with no remorse and no intention of changing the behavior, I recommend temporary separation that delivers a message that you will not tolerate that kind of repeated behavior. As long as that activity continues, you have no sexual obligation to your spouse lest you participate in an adulterous lifestyle, to say nothing of the risk of deadly sexually transmitted diseases.

Remember this: A sexual affair is not the end of a marriage, if the offender sincerely repents of his/her

---

"We are not commanded to automatically divorce because our spouse has been unfaithful."

---

sin. To be sure, it hurts, it cuts to the core, it crushes your spirit, and it deeply offends and wounds you; but it is not the end of the marriage.

But What If My Spouse Is Addicted To Pornography?

I was stunned to discover that a young man who was married in our church a few years back began bringing pornographic materials into his home to "stimulate" the sex between him and his wife. When she came to see me, she brought a whole grocery sack full of magazines, videos, pictures, and books from the world of porn. She had discovered them in the attic of his little workshop and confronted him with them. His response was that he was into pornography prior to their marriage, saw nothing wrong with it, and that he needed these things to make him a better lover. He obviously had a twisted and perverted concept of love and sex. She had the name of a Christian attorney and was leaving my office for his to file for divorce. While her husband had not committed physical adultery with other women, he had committed a form of "visual" adultery, thus sinning against his wife of only two years. She had, in fact, been told by her parents that once a person is hooked on porn, they seldom get free. I was able to confront him and guide him to the place where he felt the conviction of the Holy Spirit, repented, and asked his wife's forgiveness. It was granted, but he was not out of the woods yet. It took almost an entire year of counseling and accountability to get him free from this addiction. American people spent eight billion dollars last year on all forms of pornography. In more than half of all violent sex crimes, pornography was involved.

If your spouse is into pornography, it is not grounds for divorce, but it is grounds for confrontation. Here is where Matthew 18:15ff comes into play. Tough love demands that you serve notice on your spouse that this filth must go. It may even mean temporary separation. It definitely will mean extended biblical counseling, but thank God many people are set free from this.

But What If My Spouse Physically Abuses Me?

A Virginia policeman recently told me that more than half of all his calls have to do with domestic violence. This kind of abuse is on the increase in our country. More than half of all women murdered in this nation are murdered by their husbands. If your husband is physically violent and has shown a pattern of hitting you or your children, please remove yourself from that living situation. Physical violence is not a biblical reason for divorce, but it is reason enough for you to be protected. God does not want you exposing yourself to that destructive behavior. Secondly, your husband desperately needs biblical confrontation, especially if he claims to be a Christian. This is best done by the leadership of your church. He then needs to get into a men's discipling group where there is high accountability. Please assure him that you love him and definitely do not want the marriage to end, but neither will you tolerate that kind of repeated physical abuse.

What If My Spouse Is an Alcoholic?

There are an estimated eight million alcoholics in America today. Many of these alcoholics are married. People who have never been around alcoholics have no idea how destructive and abusive they can be when they're drunk. I can certainly see where a spouse could say, "I see no hope for my marriage as long as this drinking pattern continues." Yet we need to remember that this addiction is not biblical grounds for divorce. You married your spouse "for better or for worse." Your spouse happens to be worse right now, if he/she is an actively drinking alcoholic.

Maybe you are saying, "What do I do?" Again, there may be some situations in which physical separation must take place on a temporary basis where destructive behavior manifests itself. Secondly, do not be an "enabler." Do not make excuses for him or try to hide his sin from others. Here is where tough love comes in. You may want to do what is known as an "intervention." This is where you arrange a surprise time with your spouse to meet with family, friends, associates, and whomever he deeply respects, confront him with his problem, and insist that he immediately go into some kind of alcohol treatment center. You deliver a message that says, "We love you too much to merely stand by and watch you kill yourself and us." No, this kind of meeting is not easy, but it often works. Usually arrangements with a treatment center are made prior to the confrontation. The clothing is packed, and the car is ready. Make sure you find a Christian treatment center that makes Scripture a part of the over-all treatment.

No, you do not have to throw in the towel if your spouse is addicted to alcohol. His addiction is curable, and the marriage is worth saving.

But What If My Husband Is a Compulsive Gambler?

No one can estimate the financial devastation that is wrought on marriages and families when the breadwinner gambles all his earnings away and digs a deep hole of debt that cannot be paid back.

When there is no money to pay the bills because it has been gambled away, heavy resentments can build. Communication can be cut off, and relationships seriously impaired, if not severed. But again, I remind you, that sin is sin, whether it takes the form of drinking until you are drunk, reading or viewing pornography, committing adultery, or gambling your money away. I cannot stress enough that old fashioned *repentance* is desperately needed, along with discipleship that embraces accountability. Interventions have often been used with this sin also.

Many wives reason: *"If he won't support our family financially, I don't have a marriage."* Remember the vows . . . "in sickness and in health, in sorrow and in joy, for richer for poorer . . ." Right now it is poorer, because your husband has sinned. It appears that he does not love his family, and he may not at this point, but do not give up on him or your marriage. Gambling is not biblical grounds for divorce. You cannot justify a divorce biblically because your husband is addicted to the sin of gambling.

But What If You Are Married To Someone Who Cannot Hold a Job?

I'll call her Betty. In tears she told me that in the seven years of her marriage to Hal, he had never held a job longer than a few months. In seven years, he had been unemployed almost four and was presently unemployed. She had worked as a waitress in the evenings, earning enough for grocery money.

Their financial picture was worse than a disaster! Hal was basically lazy and irresponsible, with no sense of pride as the breadwinner. Betty had decided to file for divorce and that she would be better off financially for the courts to *make* Hal pay child support for their three year old. She felt she was "enabling" and encouraging Hal to not work by doing nothing. She was desperate. Besides this, her parents had encouraged her to divorce him, calling him a lazy bum who never intended to do anything. We put Hal in a men's discipleship group with two other men who knew the whole story.

In a sense, they "thrashed" Hal (in a good way) by showing from Scripture what his responsiblity was as a husband to provide for his family. They strongly prompted him to take some job training, which he did, and they walked him through the process of landing a responsible welding job. In this case the marriage was saved, Hal was changed, and Betty's love and respect returned to him. They are happily married today. "But," you say, "what if it hadn't worked?" There are no scriptural grounds for divorce on the basis of the fact that the husband refuses to work.

Many wives do not want to risk quitting their job, and placing the responsibility squarely on the husband's shoulders because it is too risky. I challenge you to do just that. As long as you work, you become an enabler, in spite of your good intentions. You are still "bailing" him out by continuing to work. You should definitely quit work if you have small children at home. One thing is for sure . . . it brings the crisis to a head much sooner this way and forces your spouse to deal with it. I fully realize the risks involved. But the present way is not working, and I believe God would sometimes have us "forced" to carry out our role.

But What If My Spouse Is Turned Off to Sex?

As a rule, though not always, this complaint comes from the husband about the wife. "She's frigid. . . . Surely God does not expect me to go the rest of my life without my needs being met . . . thus I believe I have a right to divorce." Sometimes the shoe is on the other foot, and it is the husband who manifests no interest at all in sex. What does the other partner do?

First of all, if there is no sexual unfaithfulness on the part of the "cold" partner, you have no biblical basis to file for divorce, none at all.

Secondly, the Bible is clear concerning sex in marriage:

> Do not deprive each other except by mutual consent and for a time, so that you may devote yourselves to prayer. Then come together again so that Satan will not tempt you because of your lack of self control. (1 Corinthians 7:5)

Earlier in that chapter Paul says: "The husband should fulfill his marital duty to his wife and likewise the wife to her husband" (1 Corinthians 7:3). Neither partner is to deprive the other of sexual fulfillment. But, having said that, remember that your first priority in marriage is to please your spouse, *not to be pleased by your spouse.* To say "I'm divorcing my spouse because my sexual needs aren't being met" is to give selfishness as a valid reason for divorce. The way to solve the problem is not to end the marriage, but to modify the marriage.

First of all, help your spouse discover the *reason* for withholding sex. Is it something that you are doing or not doing? Is it because your spouse was sexually abused earlier in life and thus creating a block against sex which is not his or her fault? Are there physical reasons?

The first key is communication. Perhaps godly counsel should be sought. Whatever measures you take, avoid just sweeping the issue under the rug and thinking it will go away. Avoid the drastic thought of divorce. Covenant to live with your spouse through this inequity until it is remedied. Remember you married "until death," not until your partner ceased to satisfy you sexually. This is not to put down sex in marriage or to relegate it to the level of non-importance, but it is to say it should never become *the* deciding issue in your marriage. Unconditional love draws a big enough circle to take that problem in.

But What If We Are Totally Incompatible?

Some feel that divorce is justifiable over being sentenced to an entire life of being opposites. The truth is that "incompatibility" can be the greatest asset in your marriage if you will simply allow it to be. I have a friend who wrote a very good book entitled, *Incompatibility: Grounds For A Great Marriage!* It is a winner, because it points out that God often links us up to an opposite to accentuate and utilize our unique giftedness. He also points to the sense of balance that two people bring to each other who have opposite interests. I remember counseling a couple who were ready to call it quits years ago. Without using names, here is their profile of likes:

He Likes	She Likes
Bright colors	Pastels
Country/Western Music	Chopin/Bach
Sports	Ballet
Traveling by plane	Traveling by car
The beach	The mountains
Sports cars	Economy cars
Coffee	Tea
Luxury items	Sale items
No children	Wants three children

He Likes	She Likes
Alcohol	Soft drinks
Lots of friends	Few friends
For her to work	To stay home

Those were just a few of their "opposites." They did not even like the same movies, hair styles, foods, or churches. In fact, they had only one thing in common. They both disliked everything the other liked!

Incompatibility is not grounds for divorce, but rather an opportunity for couples to prove that opposites cannot only attract each other, but can complement each other.

But What If My Spouse Is Serving a Long-term Prison Sentence?

I once counseled a young woman about twenty-eight years old whose husband had been sent to the state prison for a twenty-four years sentence with the possibility for parole in nine years. She asked me if she could legally divorce him according to the Bible. The answer was no, to which she blurted out, "It isn't fair, I have to spend the young years of my life without a husband." I reminded her that we live in a fallen world where many things appear to not be fair. I also reminded her that she married him, knowing he had a previous record. Though he had professed Christ before they were married, his behavior did not seem to demonstrate that. We must live with our choices, but what we really want is the privilege of violating biblical principle without the negative circumstances. We cannot do both.

What is the answer? You made a vow, you keep your vow. Not only stay married to him, but love him, pray for him, and encourage him.

"Incompatibility is not grounds for divorce, but rather an opportunity for couples to prove that opposites cannot only attract each other, but can complement each other."

In essence, there is no excuse for a divorce. Marriage is a commitment. It is not a mushy feeling of romance and love. It is rather a sealed vow that says you are committed to that one person for as long as they live.

Why not get to your knees right now, and make a new commitment of your life to your marriage. Read this prayer out loud:

Dear God, thank you for (spouse's name). I recommit affection and loyalty to (spouse's name) right now. Show me, Lord, where I have erred. I also rededicate my life to You. In Jesus' name, Amen.

EPILOGUE

As I write these lines, my mind races back over the years to an elderly couple who for years now have been in heaven. When I was only nineteen years old, they hosted me every weekend in a small town in central Alabama where I preached. Charles and Beulah Myhand cherished a marriage that had survived at that time for fifty-seven years. They were seasoned. On chilly winter evenings around the fire, they told me of the early days of their marriage. They were married in the early 1900's before the existence of washing machines, dryers, electric stoves, dishwashers, television, and in their case, radios. They both came from very poor families. Charles' parents combined farming and school teaching. Beulah's parents died when she was young, and she was raised by relatives. As a young man not even thinking of marriage, I was still enthralled to sit and listen to what they went through in just the first two or three years of their marriage. Bad health, the loss of two babies, jobless, and constantly moving, they had enough liabilities to throw in the towel and bail out. But they did not. Charles looked me straight in the eye and said, "Young man, there are three essential ingredients to staying married till God calls one of you home." I waited to hear what this wise old man would say.

"First," he said, "there's devotion . . . we were devoted to each other, and refused to allow anything or anyone to alter that devotion. Secondly . . . there's trust, 100 percent trust, and it's not a feeling either, it's a fact. Thirdly, and most important, hard work. We worked at having a good relationship, and when we saw it slipping, we worked harder."

I'll never forget that elderly couple. I watched them hold hands on Sunday as they sat in church. I saw him open the door on their old car and help her get in. He had done that for more than fifty-seven years. I saw them grin at each other in their home . . . you could sense the romance; it was thick! They never lost the wonder of their relationship. Only a year after I was last in their home, Charles was killed in an auto accident very close to his home. Beulah said, "Part of me left with him, and I'll never be the same." She mourned herself to death within the next year. What a couple, what a marriage!

As my mind races back to those scenes some thirty-five years ago, I muse: Most couples who file for divorce today have not been through a fraction of the pain, poverty, disappointment, and heartache Charles and Beulah had endured, yet they are willing to throw in the towel.

I have taken Charles' three "essential ingredients" into my own marriage of thirty-three years. My wife and I have stayed devoted. We refuse to allow circumstances to pull us away from each other and are determined that we will allow nothing to be bigger than our devotion to each other.

We have also nurtured trust. No marriage will survive long without trust, implicit trust. Neither of us has tried to "control" or "monitor" the other. Nor have we tried to remake each other into someone else. We have not always understood each other's idiosyncrasies, but we have trusted each other through it all. Finally, we have worked at keeping our marriage strong. I once had a small garden. No one told me it had to be weeded regularly. The weeds completely overtook the entire plot, and I lost my garden. Upkeep is not automatic in a garden or in a marriage. We have tried to keep our arguments few, our make-up period swift, and have made sure that when we went to bed there were no grudges pending.

Has it been easy? No. There are times in every marriage when the thought crosses your mind to perhaps leave the marriage. Don't! It is not worth it. You will regret the day you made the decision. It is better to tough it out, work at it, and live with a mate who has imperfections than to throw in the towel. Someone once said: *"The bonds of matrimony are a good investment only when the interest is kept up."* Don't lose the interest. Work at your marriage and make it a priority above all else.

In conclusion, before you file for divorce, take the following steps:

- *Forgive your spouse.* Your spouse may have sinned greatly against you, but failure to forgive only weaves a web that will bind you a cripple. Go to your spouse and say, "I want you to know that I forgive you for what you've done."

- *Visualize what your lives can be together.* Do not focus on the present but on the future. Do not think about what your marriage is like now; think about what God can make it to be in the future. Recall those early days when your relationship together was powerful, before the devil muddied the water between you.

- *Consider what God wants in this situation, not what you want.* It is so easy to initiate a divorce because you feel it is what you want, and that it will somehow solve some problems. Of course divorce never solves problems, it only creates them. Seek to please the Lord, not your own desires. Get on your knees and ask God, "Do you want me to divorce my spouse?"

- *Humble yourself before your mate.* I know this is asking almost the impossible, but until you humble yourself and acknowledge your *own* downfall and inadequacies, there will be nothing to build on.

- *Do not give up!* Do not back away from standing up for the healing of your marriage. Remember, your relationship is not built on warm, fuzzy feelings or some "euphoria" of romance, but it is built on commitment. Determine to make that commitment, pay the price, and do what God wants most. Remember again, God said, "I hate divorce" (Malachi 2:16). Decide now that you will hate what God hates!

A Prayer for Strength

Lord, I humble myself before You . . . and before my mate. Forgive my thoughts of revenge and bitterness. Enable me to stand for this marriage and thus glorify You. Assist me now to do the godly thing, the biblical thing, the right thing, to refuse to file for the dissolution of my marriage. I pray blessings today upon my spouse. I pray that You turn his/her bitter thoughts about me into love again. Thank You, Lord, for the victory that I know is coming! Amen.

SUBJECT INDEX

SCRIPTURE INDEX

— *ABOUT THE AUTHOR*

B ob Moorehead has been preaching for thirty-five years, twenty-two of which as pastor of Overlake Christian Church, Kirkland, WA, attended by over six thousand people. He and Glenita have enjoyed thirty-three years of marriage that produced three children, two of which are in full-time ministry.

Bob writes out of a deep conviction that the covenant of marriage is not only a warm relationship between man and wife but a binding relationship that was never meant to be severed, no matter what, except by death.

This is his third book on marriage and his sixth book altogether. He strongly believes the destiny of our nation lies in the strength of our marriages and homes.

A Manufacturing Guide
To Good Husbanding

The Husband Handbook:
Essentials for Growing a Healthy Marriage
Dr. Bob Moorehead
ISBN: 0-943497-43-4
Trade Paper, 176 pages
Love and Marriage

EVERY MAJOR APPLIANCE COMES WITH a handbook filled with everything you'd ever want to know about them. Top to bottom, inside and out. How they work and what they're made of.

What if these same manuals were available to couples, helping them to better understand their marriage relationship?

Dr. Bob Moorehead's book is just that: *a relationship manual.* He calls *The Husband Handbook*, the "manufacturer's guide to good husbanding." It's a complete description of what makes a successful husband biblically. This book is filled with practical suggestions ready to be applied, helping every man to better understand what his wife needs and what God expects.

Dr. Moorehead is a pastor, psychologist, and the author of the bestselling book, *The Marriage Repair Kit.*

For Further Reading

Small Repairs That Can Make a Big Difference

"Most marriages are in need of simple repair, not total renovation."

THE MARRIAGE REPAIR KIT

Dr. Bob Moorehead

The Marriage Repair Kit
Dr. Bob Moorehead
ISBN: 0-943497-30-2
Trade Paper, 192 pages
Marriage/Family

MOST MARRIAGES ARE IN NEED OF SIMPLE repair not total renovation. In this very practical book, pastor and author Bob Moorehead shows how to make those small adjustments that can make a big difference in any marriage. Covering virtually every subject from communication to recreation, from the bedroom to the checkbook, and from the family's spiritual walk to the children's emotional drain, he provides clear instructions on how to make strong marriages even stronger.

Bob Moorehead, Ph.D., is the senior pastor of Overlake Christian Church in Kirkland, Washington. He and Glenita, his wife of thirty years, have three children.

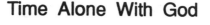

Time Alone With God

QuieTimes: A Complete, Day-By-Day Guide
To Personal Worship and Bible Study
Max E. Anders
ISBN: 0-943497-45-0
Hard Cover, 380 pages
Devotional

IN THIS BOOK ARE 365 COMPLETE GUIDES for your time alone with God. Each day there is a suggested Scripture passage, key chapters for an understanding of basic Bible doctrine or significant biblical events, an opportunity to reflect on what has just been read, and, then a guided opportunity for a personal response to the Lord.

Dr. Max Anders, the author of *30 Days to Understanding the Bible, 30 Days to Understanding the Christian Life,* and coauthor of *30 Days to Understanding Church History* is the pastor of Grace Covenant Church in Austin, Texas.

A Book for the Man Who Knows More About Football Than Marriage

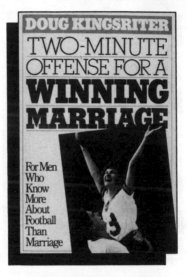

Two-Minute Offense for a Winning Marriage:
For Men Who Know More About
Football Than Marriage
Doug Kingsriter
ISBN: 0-943497-59-0
Hard Cover, 116 pages
Marriage

HERE, AT LAST, IS A BOOK ON MARRIAGE FOR MEN—men who know a lot more about football than they do about marriage.

Doug Kingsriter, a former professional football player himself, very cleverly uses a football game, the quarterback, the line, the coach, and the opposition as an analogy to teach men what their role should be as husbands and fathers, and their God-appointed responsibility to properly care and lead their homes.

This is a fresh, new approach to marriage that every man will thoroughly understand.